Santa Claus Is Alive and Well and Living on Wall Street

Also by Bruce Gauthier, as bruce.fm

Music Albums:
2001 While I'm Still Alive Vol. 1—Ambient
2001 While I'm Still Alive Vol. 2—Pop
2001 While I'm Still Alive Vol. 3—The Reluctant Clairvoyant
2002 acid b.rain
2002 All You Have to Do Is Believe
2003 fragile life
2004 Beauty Is Mesmerizing
2005 Convenience
2006 Centrebration

Santa Claus Is Alive and Well and Living on Wall Street

Spoiler Alert—This Is Not a Children's Story!

Bruce Gauthier

iUniverse, Inc.
Bloomington

Santa Claus Is Alive and Well and Living on Wall Street
Spoiler Alert—This Is Not a Children's Story!

Copyright © 2011 by Bruce Gauthier

All rights reserved. No part of this book may be used or reproduced by any means, graphic, electronic, or mechanical, including photocopying, recording, taping or by any information storage retrieval system without the written permission of the publisher except in the case of brief quotations embodied in critical articles and reviews.

iUniverse books may be ordered through booksellers or by contacting:

iUniverse
1663 Liberty Drive
Bloomington, IN 47403
www.iuniverse.com
1-800-Authors (1-800-288-4677)

Because of the dynamic nature of the Internet, any web addresses or links contained in this book may have changed since publication and may no longer be valid. The views expressed in this work are solely those of the author and do not necessarily reflect the views of the publisher, and the publisher hereby disclaims any responsibility for them.

Any people depicted in stock imagery provided by Thinkstock are models, and such images are being used for illustrative purposes only.

Certain stock imagery © Thinkstock.

ISBN: 978-1-4620-1228-2 (sc)
ISBN: 978-1-4620-1229-9 (hc)
ISBN: 978-1-4620-1230-5 (e)

Library of Congress Control Number: 2011907031

Printed in the United States of America

iUniverse rev. date: 07/05/2011

Dedicated to Hughie, Ken, Burford, my dad, and all the others who have passed before me but continue to give me good advice. Kisses and hugs to my family and friends who have supported me through this diatribe.

"Watching Christians do Christmas is like watching hippies take drugs."

—*Jeffrey Paul, my soul-crazy photography teacher from Sheridan College*

Table of Contents

Introduction 1
1. Santa Claus: The Early Years 4
2. Santa Claus Is Alive and Well and Living on Wall Street 8
3. "There Is No Sanity Clause!" 17
4. Manipulation and Disinformation 22
5. The Wolves Are Guarding the Henhouse 26
6. Fixing the Mess 33
7. Give Us Our Jobs Back 36
8. Cost Cutting 48
9. Volume and Saturation 56
10. Outsourcing 65
11. Stock Options, or Legal Counterfeiting 97
12. "The Root of All Evil" 115
13. "Confusion Will be My Epitaph" 131
About the Author 135
Appendix A: Larry Summers Testimony July 1998 137
Appendix B: The Original Preface for This Book
              from April, 2009 147
Bibliography 149

Introduction

This book is about the absurdities that come from trying to make sense of a financial world that was supposed to be making a retirement nest egg for me.

I wrote the beginnings of this book back in March of 2009 and finished the first draft at the end of April 2009, when my wife made me stop writing and concentrate on getting our taxes finished in order to meet the tax deadline. The original introduction is now Appendix B at the back of this book.

I felt the need to rewrite this introduction for one reason: twenty months later, in December of 2010, not much has changed in the financial crisis. There are debates going on about whether the recession has ended, but it seems now that most are in agreement that it hasn't. Now it seems that the "experts" on Wall Street have realized that unemployment actually may be the reason we can't seem to get out of this recession—and that the toxic assets Wall Street sold to unsuspecting investors were not a bad risk but in fact, as Joshua Rosner, managing director at independent research consultancy Graham Fisher & Co., told the *Huffington Post*, "a massive fraud perpetrated on the investing public on a scale never before seen."[1]

I have had the opportunity to hear the CEOs of Fortune 500 companies speak to their employees and customers, and have been

---

1 Shahien Nasiripour, "New Proof Wall Street Knew Its Mortgage Securities Were Subpar: Clayton Execs Testify," *Huffington Post*, September 25, 2010, http://www.huffingtonpost.com/2010/09/25/wall-street-subprime-crisis_n_739294.html.

behind the scenes with them as they fake their demos, manipulate their speeches, and craft their PowerPoint© slides with the fervor of implementing a NASA shuttle launch. "We can't say this, we can't say that … The street will kill us if we say that …" This type of message manipulation is only the tip of the iceberg when it comes to the shenanigans that I will address in my book. And if you've never heard the expression "Death by PowerPoint©," then try sitting in a boardroom with a group of nervous executives for four hours as they try to phrase a single PowerPoint© slide! Or as I heard one executive put it, "You're worried about million dollar decisions, while we're worried about billion dollar decisions."

This book is written from the point of view of someone who has ignored investing and stock markets all of his life, expecting someone else to look after his financial good. This was my first mistake. Second, no one told me that my 401K (or, in Canada, an RRSP) could actually *lose* value. *Caveat emptor*—"let the buyer beware," for those who hate foreign phrases they can't understand, ultimately meaning that you are responsible for what you buy, and you should know the pitfalls before making a commitment or investment.

I decided to pursue publishing this book late in 2010 because it is still relevant for those of us who are angry and feel somewhat helpless against the thieves who have found legal ways to get our money out of our retirement savings plans and into their pockets. Helpless, that is, until I took my money out of that high-risk stock market and put it somewhere more stable, like gold.

The premise of this book is that there is a direct correlation between being raised as a child believing in Santa Claus and being an adult believing that the stock market is going to have nice big gifts on our own adult version of Christmas Day: retirement day!

This book is not for financiers, brokers, investment advisers, or anyone who has an "in" with Wall Street. This book is written for the people like me who trust others to take care of building our retirement savings, those of us who have little knowledge of the inner workings of the financial world.

Note: Bruce Gauthier is not a Registered Investment Adviser and therefore is not licensed to give trading advice of any sort or make specific trading recommendations. This book is for educational purposes and is the personal opinion of the author. The author's opinion is not meant to be construed as an invitation or solicitation to trade. For trading advice, consult your broker or licensed investment adviser. Or find a nice bottle of wine and have a glass and wonder what the rich people did with your money.

Chapter 1
Santa Claus: The Early Years

I was the youngest of six kids. For much of my childhood, I was the typical "Santa!" believer. I had faith in Santa Claus to make my dreams come true.

But like any good fantasy, it couldn't last. The unraveling of my belief in Santa started in 1967 in second grade thanks to a schoolmate named Steve who didn't believe in Santa Claus. He was in my brother's grade, one year ahead of me. About a week out from Christmas, my brother Jim and I were standing with Steve at recess, discussing what Santa was going to bring us.

Jim nodded toward Steve and said to me, "Did you know that Steve doesn't believe in Santa? And he doesn't get any presents?" *Horrors!* I knew that if you *did* believe in Santa Claus, you got presents. But it never occurred to me that if you *didn't* believe in Santa Claus …

As each year passed, more and more of my schoolmates would suggest that Santa Claus did not exist, and that I was a sucker for believing in Santa. *My Santa Claus?!? Does not exist?!? How could that be?* Like every good questioning child, I would ask those in authority, the ones I trusted to give me honest and complete answers—my mother, sisters, and brothers. I would ask them for *the truth!*

I knew better than to ask my dad. My dad would just say, "Go ask your mother," so there was no sense bothering to ask him. (*Can I get you another beer, Dad?*)

And so they told me what I wanted to hear. "Of course Santa

Claus is real. Your friends have just been bad, and you know that Santa doesn't bring presents to children who are bad." That was the answer I was looking for!

Let's pause here to ask the question, "What age is a good age to admit the truth to a child questioning Santa's existence?"

When I was in my late twenties, I was at a social function and ran into a married couple I hadn't seen since their wedding. The wife was a teacher, and she told me that she had come up with the idea of having the second-grade students write letters to Santa Claus, and then her sixth-grade students would write back to the second-graders as if the sixth-graders *were* Santa Claus.

The plan backfired when it turned out that several of the sixth-grade students still believed in Santa Claus, and their parents were now very unhappy that their children had to find out *the truth!*

I said to the teacher, "To be honest, I think it is a sign of the failure of our educational system to have twelve-year-old people who do not understand the flaws in the Santa Claus theory"—flying reindeer; visiting every child in the world in one night; coming down chimneys; elves making gifts for Hasbro; a Santa in every mall; and so on.

The teacher took great offence. She felt that it was not the responsibility of the educational system to make sure that by the age of twelve, a student has a clear enough understanding of reality to be able to figure out that Santa Claus is a myth.

Our discussion became quite loud and heated, and attracted much attention at the party. I haven't spoken to her since.

This was a turning point for me in the way I viewed parenting and the way I reflected on things that happened in my childhood that made me who I am today. I don't necessarily mean that in a positive sense.

I have a very good friend who decided that she would get pregnant without telling her common-law spouse. Yes, her spouse could have taken action to prevent this from happening. But we like to assume that trust is a part of every relationship.

She is one of those people who wanted her sneakily conceived son to believe in Santa Claus for as long as possible, perhaps until university. The merits of "extending" the belief in Santa Claus well past a reasonable amount of time became discussion fodder for the two of us. If I remember correctly, her excuse was, "I want my kid to have what I didn't get as a child!"

Like many other mothers I have spoken to, she had never taken into consideration the other part of her child's life, the part where the kids at school are making fun of him because he still believes in Santa Claus at the ripe old age of twelve, just like me.

The bullying, the razzing, the being made a fool of in front of your peers, in front of the girls—*in front of the girls!!!* Holy crap! No guy wants to be made fun of in front of *the girls!* What will Mary-Anne think of me now? Mary-Anne was my unrequited love until we went our separate ways after Grade 8, although I did ask her to dance at the prom.

Much like the character in the song "(The Only Gay) Eskimo" by Corky and the Juice Pigs, I was now "The Only Child Left in Sixth Grade Who Still Believes in Santa!" This can be a lonely and frustrating place.

A few years ago, in the lobby bar of the St. Francis Hotel in San Francisco, I listened as the three women I was working with discussed their children, nieces, nephews, and grandchildren, relative to the approaching Christmas.

The common theme was the kick, or the high, or the satisfaction that they achieved by putting on, much like a Broadway producer, the perfect Christmas morning for the kids. Apparently the success of this act was measured by the look on the kids' faces as they saw and opened the presents left behind by Santa—and these parents and grandparents now had the video to prove it. The child's excited look! The child's thrilled face! The look of satisfaction that Santa had given them *everything they asked for!* And the parents and grandparents got to stand up and yell, "*I'm the gold medal winner at the Parenting Olympics!*"

There was no Parenting Olympics at my house. We lived off of my father's meager salary. Mom gave birth to six kids in nine years. There was not a lot of money to put up a very good Christmas Parenting Olympics presentation.

So in our house, it was "The child's look of disappointment!" and "The child's look of despair!" and "The child's look of ..." I had better take it easy on myself here—this is digging up some bad memories. To be fair to my mom, at least it wasn't bags of coal.

My parents tried hard. And my grandmother usually came through with "the big gift," something a little more expensive than the "almost what we asked for" toys that Mom and Santa left for us.

Now let's go back to the lobby bar of the St. Francis Hotel in San Francisco.

The topic of the belief in Santa Claus came up again (as it does whenever I am given the chance), and these women confirmed the reasoning behind their motivation. Just like my friend, they wanted their children to have the best, to have what they didn't have.

I brought up the other side of the coin—the kids at school making fun of their child for the errant belief in Santa Claus—and I capped it with this observation:

"So here I am at the age of twelve, the only kid left in my class still believing in Santa Claus, because the authorities I look to told me that it was *the truth*, and I'm being ridiculed, persecuted, being made fun of in front of the girls, and then finally, I am told the truth. And my first reaction is—*why have you been lying to me all of this time?!?*"

There was a bit of silence in the lobby bar. I went on to explain how I still live with this distrust of authority, brought on by the people I loved and trusted who had been *lying* to me for, really, their own satisfaction. I've now got a wedge jammed in my heart, causing me pain that may not ever go away, because someone wanted to pull me along for their own amusement. *Those selfish bastards!*

And once I realized that I had been lied to, the consequences started flooding through my feeble brain—the embarrassing realization that your schoolmates think you are one giant baby. How could I ever get a date with Mary-Anne? No one is ever going to take me seriously! *I must be the laughingstock of the entire school!*

I was afraid to go to sleep that night, because I knew I would have to wake up in the morning and face the terrible people who had been lying to me and the terrible people who had been making fun of me, and how could I ever look Mary-Anne in the eyes again? I had a hollow feeling in the pit of my stomach, and I thought I was going to puke. It was the first time I ever had a suicidal thought.

There in the lobby bar of the St. Francis Hotel, the ladies looked up from their cocktails and thoughtfully said, "I've never looked at it that way."

"You better not pout, you better not squirm,
This pervert is holding you firm,
Santa Claus is going to town!"

Chapter 2
Santa Claus Is Alive and Well and Living on Wall Street

When I was first told about investing in 401Ks (or as they're called in Canada, RRSPs), the premise was this: If I put little gifts of money under the Christmas tree and wait patiently until Christmas day (when I retire), then someone named Santa Claus (living on Wall Street) will have added a whole bunch of presents (read: more money) under the tree, and when I wake up (on retirement day) and go running down the stairs in the morning into the living room and look under the tree, all those presents will be mine! *Fantastic!*

Or so it seems. This is the basic premise that Wall Street works upon. If you put little bits of money away now, those bits will, apparently by magic, grow into larger bits of money for you to have further down the road. This premise is called "investing."

But now, let's imagine that there are a group of people obsessed with getting your money out of the stock market. To what lengths will they go to get that money while people like you and I sit back and say, "Oh, apparently there's a recession"? We rarely hear anyone say, "Those bastards just took a trillion dollars out of the stock market!" This may be closer to the truth than we would like to think.

If this suspect element has some control over the media, and the

SEC, and an undetermined but significant number of traders on Wall Street, then it may be possible that what we see as "volatility in the stock market" is actually the result of a carefully planned and executed manipulation that puts millions upon millions of dollars into their pockets while draining our retirement funds.

In the media, it would be important that the faces of Wall Street give us the impression that all is well to keep us, the people putting the cash into the stock market, still investing—still believing in Santa Claus.

My belief in Santa Claus living on Wall Street is over. There is no Santa Claus. There is just a bunch of people who have figured out both how to fool you into thinking you are investing and how to remove your money from the system and make it seem like it wasn't their fault. Some methods of removing your money are illegal, but that is not what this book is about. The methods discussed here are dubious at best but perfectly legal. Or shall we say—legal to the point that the perpetrators still haven't been indicted. Nobel-prize-winning author Paul Krugman weighs in:

> Americans are angry at Wall Street, and rightly so. First the financial industry plunged us into economic crisis, then it was bailed out at taxpayer expense. If you aren't outraged, you haven't been paying attention.
>
> But crashing the economy and fleecing the taxpayer aren't Wall Street's only sins. Even before the crisis and the bailouts, many financial-industry high-fliers made fortunes through activities that were worthless if not destructive from a social point of view.[2]

These are the methods that concern me. Whenever it comes to laws being made, there are people who will immediately set out to find a way to get around the system, or better yet, get laws changed to make what was once an illegal activity legal. Any time there is a large pile of "pleasure" to be had—be it a large pile of money, drugs, prostitution, or gambling—the large pile of pleasure is going to attract those who

---

2   Paul Krugman, "Rewarding Bad Actors," *New York Times*, August 2, 2009, http://www.nytimes.com/2009/08/03/opinion/03krugman.html.

want to benefit from the general public's obsession with it. This book is about the pleasure that can be derived from the stock market.

Let me suggest an interesting analogy to the way the stock market works. I want you to picture in your mind a tall grain silo with a conveyor belt reaching to the top, dropping grains of wheat into the bottom of the silo. What happens when the grain keeps coming and the conveyor never stops? The silo gets full. Now imagine that each grain of wheat is one of your investment dollars. Beware the thousands of people, if not tens of thousands of people, who want to find ways to make sure that the grain silo never gets full and have found ways to remove the grain (your money) for their own benefit. The bonus for these thieves, legal or otherwise, is that we, the investors, keep the conveyor belt full, insuring a constant influx of grain (money) into the silo. Do you have automatic payroll deduction putting your hard-earned dollars onto the conveyor belt?

The problem we have is trying to figure out who is genuine and who wants us to keep believing in Santa Claus.

We've all looked for a guiding light—someone who can tell us where to invest our money. Television and the Internet are full of "experts" who now act surprised that the recession has hit with this type of impact on the economy.

These "experts" on Wall Street are the ones who I think *still believe that Santa Claus is living on Wall Street.* They certainly don't want to be told that *there is no Santa Claus living on Wall Street!* Or at the very least, they want you to keep believing in the Santa Claus who lives on Wall Street. That way, you will keep putting money under the tree for them to take out for their benefit, not yours.

But like Steve from when I was in second grade who knew there was no Santa Claus, there were some naysayers who saw the financial collapse coming—in fine detail—but were shouted down everywhere: in the press, on TV, on the web. These naysayers knew there was no Santa Claus and were shouting it from the rooftops.

One of those naysayers was Peter Schiff. He took a lot of heat in 2006 for his belief that a recession was coming, and that it was going to be bad. Schiff went head to head with some of the best, and you can relate if you've ever been the lone soul at one end of a debate being heckled by a mob at the other end of the debate. Deep down inside, you know you are right.

Here is a transcript from an August 2006 episode of the CNBC financial news show *Kudlow & Company*, with Schiff being interviewed along with Arthur Laffer, a former adviser to President Reagan, who doesn't believe anything Schiff says:

> **Host**: Peter, I want to start with you. Although there are more and more people saying that the US economy will be in a recession next year, it is still a minority position. Why do you think that a recession is coming, and just how bad is it going to be?
>
> **Peter Schiff**: I think it's going to be pretty bad. Whether it starts in '07 or '08 I think is immaterial, and I also think it's going to last, not just for [fiscal] quarters, but for years. See, the basic problem with the US economy is we have too much consumption and borrowing, and not enough production and savings. And what's going to happen is the American consumer is basically going to stop consuming and start rebuilding his savings, especially when he sees his home equity evaporate, and when you have the economy as 70 percent consumption, you can't address those imbalances without a recession. You know, rather than the recession being resisted, it should really be embraced, because the disease is all this debt-financed consumption. The cure is that we stop consuming and start saving and producing again, and that's a recession. Sometimes, you know, medicine tastes bad, but you've got to swallow it.
>
> **Host**: Art Laffer, [do] you hear him? He says the consumer is going to slow down in order to rebuild the savings. And you know that two-thirds of the American economy is driven by the consumer. Do you believe that?

Art Laffer: No, I don't believe any of it whatsoever, Michelle. Excuse me, but what he is saying is that savings is way down in this country. But wealth has risen dramatically; the United States economy has never been in better shape; there is no tax increase coming in the next couple of years; monetary policy is spectacular; we have freer trade than ever before; and not only that, but there are no income's policies things here; I think Peter is just totally off base, and I don't think it's going to be ... I mean, I just don't know where he's getting his stuff.

Peter Schiff: [*Interrupting*] One of us is off base, but it's definitely not me. I mean, it's not wealth that's increased in the last few years; we haven't increased our productive capacity. All that's increased is the paper values of our stocks and real estate. But that's not real wealth, no more than ...

Art Laffer: [*Interrupting*] Of course it is!

Peter Schiff: When you see the stock market come down and the real-estate bubble burst, all that phony wealth is going to evaporate, and all that's going to be left is all the debt that we've accumulated to foreigners ...

Art Laffer: Peter, I'm going to make a bet with you on this one ...[3]

As Schiff predicted, the recession started. People were saving—which really means "scared to spend." The stock market came down, and the real-estate bubble burst.

Here is a transcript from a Fox News segment from December 31, 2006, where Schiff is up against three other "experts" on Wall Street:

---

3 Peter Schiff, interview on *Kudlow & Company*, CNBC, August 28, 2006, accessed November 13, 2010, http://www.europac.net/media/tv_interviews/peter_schiff_august_28_2006_cnbc.

Host: Big question—will homes be worth more or less in 2007? Tom, what do you think?

Tom Adkins: New Year's Eve—prices will go up about 10 percent, and here's why. Because you're going to come into a regular normal market, and a regular normal market—that's about what kind of appreciation you get.

Host: Home prices going to go up 10 percent in the coming year. Peter, what do you say?

Peter Schiff: Well, today's home prices are completely unsustainable. They were bid up to these artificial heights by a combination of temporarily low adjustment-rate mortgage [ARM] payments; by a complete ... absence of any lending standards; and by speculative buying. And what is going to happen in 2007 is a lot of these artificially low ARM payments are going to be reset upward. You're going to start to see both the government and the lenders reimposing lending standards and tightening up on credit. And you're going to see a lot of these speculative buyers turn into sellers. And these sky-high real-estate prices are going to come crashing back down to earth.

Mike Norman: First, I have no idea what Peter Schiff is talking about. I agree with Tom ... [*to Peter*] What artificial lending standard are you talking about?[4]

As Schiff predicted, housing prices plummeted, and it was discovered that lending standards were dubious at best.

Here is a transcript from another 2006 Fox News segment, "More for your Money," where Schiff is put up against actor, political speechwriter, and financial expert Ben Stein, former host of Comedy Central's *Win Ben Stein's Money*:

---

4   Peter Schiff, interview on Fox News, December 31, 2006, accessed March 19, 2009.

Host: Ben Stein, you say this could be a perfect storm for buyers. What do you mean?

Ben Stein: I mean that the credit crunch is way overblown ... The subprime problem is a problem, but it's a tiny problem in the context of this economy ... Meanwhile, it's as if nuclear war has struck the financials and really struck the whole market. It's a buying opportunity, especially for the financials, maybe that I've never seen before in my entire life.

Peter Schiff: This is just getting started. It's not just subprime. This is a problem for the entire mortgage industry. It's not just people with bad credit that committed to mortgages they can't afford. It's not just people with bad credit who are going to see their home equity vanish, and it's not limited to mortgage credit. Americans are going to have a difficult time borrowing money to buy cars, to buy furniture, to buy appliances. Foreigners around the world have been lending us money for years. They're now finding out that we can't afford to repay. This is going to be an enormous credit crunch. The party is over for the United States. We cannot continue borrowing to live beyond our means and consuming foreign products.

Ben Stein: Subprime is tiny. Subprime is a tiny, tiny blip.

Peter Schiff: It's not tiny, and again, it's not just subprime. It's the entire mortgage market.

Ben Stein: You're simply wrong about that ... I think stocks will be a heck of a lot higher a year from now than they are now ... Peter, do you think razor blades are in order?[5]

---

5   Peter Schiff, interview on "More for Your Money," Fox News, circa 2006, accessed March 19, 2009.

In case you don't know, stocks went a lot *lower*.

Here is a transcript from a different 2006 episode of *More for your Money*, with Stein and other "experts" on Wall Street up against Schiff. He had been warning people not to buy stock in the major financial companies (this was just prior to the collapse and bailouts). Listen to what the "experts" had to say against Peter's view:

> **Ben Stein**: Well, the financials, as I keep saying, are just super bargains. I predict that ... Merrill Lynch, which is an astonishingly well-run company ... a couple of days ago it was trading at barely more than seven times earnings ... this is a joke. This stock, they may as well be putting it in cereal boxes and giving it away, that's how cheap it is.
>
> **Host**: Charles, what do you think of that?
>
> **Charles Payne**: Yeah, I like the financials, too. Merrill isn't my top pick in a group. I think Bear [Stearns] is probably the cheapest, although the riskiest, and some of the others are better, but you know, the financials are a great place, absolutely.
>
> **Unidentified Woman**: I, again, like Ben, like the financials. I like Goldman Sachs. It's like getting Dolce & Gabbana on sale. This is the crème de la crème of Wall Street. It's cheap ... It is down, and it's probably actually gonna go further, and I think that people should start nibbling at this thing.
>
> **Peter Schiff**: Stay away from the financials, they're toxic. They're not cheap, they're expensive ... [*Uttered dismay from the other guests*] You think they're at low PEs [price-to-earnings ratio]; they have no earnings, their earnings are going to disappear.

Ben Stein: They have no earnings? Their earnings are huge!

Peter Schiff: Last year, when people were recommending home builders, and they were talking about their five or six times earnings, I said those earnings are fantasy, they're not going to be here ... [*Uttered dismay from the other guests*] There's a lot of losses coming up in the future. These financials are going to get hit, and they're going to get hit hard.

Host: Peter, I wish we had more time with you. I know you're going to want to continue that exposé on Santa Claus ...[6]

I would like to utilize an old Hungarian saying that loosely translated means, "There's the owl telling the sparrow it has a big head!" Who are the ones believing in Santa Claus? As we now know, Schiff was correct when he said that the financials had no earnings; a lot of losses did come; and the financials got hit hard. It really made me laugh when the woman said, "It's like getting Dolce & Gabbana on sale ..." Counterfeit Dolce & Gabbana, perhaps.

---

6   Peter Schiff, interview on "More for Your Money," Fox News, circa 2006, accessed March 19, 2009.

Chapter 3
"There Is No Sanity Clause!"

There is an existential philosophy that says, "There are two types of people in this world—those who believe there are two types of people in the world and those who don't." Well, I believe there are two types of "experts" on Wall Street. There are those who still believe in Santa Claus and those who know that Santa doesn't exist but don't want *you* to know that Santa doesn't exist, because that would ruin their ability to take your gifts out from under the tree for their own keeping. If they are going to get rich *or richer*, they need someone to supply the money. So if they can keep you believing that Santa Claus is alive and well and living on Wall Street, then you become their financial lifeline, their blood donor, their gift giver, their mule. So who is the Santa Claus living on Wall Street?

I once had a boss, Gary, who owned two Mercedes-Benz cars. Gary loved to tell you how he bought his first Mercedes with the winnings from a windfall on the stock market.

It is stories like this that keep people like Gary believing that Santa Claus is alive and well and living on Wall Street—Gary put his money under the Christmas tree, and Santa came through big time! Remember the first time you were old enough to really appreciate it when Santa gave you exactly what you asked for? And at that point, there was no doubting Santa's existence.

Now that Gary had experienced the "Wall Street Santa" effect, he would be a firm believer in Santa forever. No one was ever going to convince him that it was a bad idea. If he did it once, he could do it again. This tends to be the creed of people with gambling problems—did I just say "gambling problems"?!? Matt Taibbi comments with this remark, as published in the March 19, 2009 issue of *Rolling Stone*:

> Nor did anyone mention that when AIG finally got up from its seat at the Wall Street casino, broke and busted in the afterdawn light, it owed money all over town—and that a huge chunk of your taxpayer dollars in this particular bailout scam will be going to pay off the other high rollers at its table. Or that this was a casino unique among all casinos, one where middle-class taxpayers cover the bets of billionaires.[7]

There have been stock winning streaks in the '70s, '80s, and '90s where big wins happened to many people I know. And who can forget the investors in Trivial Pursuit or Microsoft or any of those stories where small investments paid off more than handsomely for risk-taking people. Risk-taking is a human trait that some will indulge, but only a few will come out winners.

Many people feel that the stock market is a solid, logical place to invest money, in much the same way that some prefer belief in the Darwin theory of evolution versus a belief in God (large "G" out of respect)—because it seems logical and makes sense to them.

So where does it all go wrong? How is it that I would have better invested my money in empty-beer-bottle refunds than Enron? How is it that the "experts" on Wall Street can make mistakes so profound that they wipe out a decade of investing and threaten the heart and soul of a country? More conveniently phrased, "How could they get it so wrong?"

Let's discuss what we do know. On Black Monday in October of

---

7   Matt Taibbi, "The Big Takeover," Rolling Stone, March 19, 2009, accessed March 19, 2009, http://www.rollingstone.com/politics/story/26793903/the_big_takeover/print.

1987, during the bottoming out of the market in 2001 and 2002, and in recent months at the end of 2008, large amounts of money were either taken out of the stock market or "just disappeared," effectively depleting the retirement portfolios of those about to retire and greatly diminishing investments for those new to investing.

I looked through my retirement investment statements until I found the year that my investments were worth what they're worth now. That year was 2002. So in effect, I lost eight years of investing. Meanwhile, my wife, who has everything invested in Guaranteed Income Certificates (GICs), got her statement and said, "Wow, I didn't lose a thing!" It may have only been 3.5 percent, but that was better than losing everything from the last seven years of investing. One financier said to me, "Some people's investments are back to 1997 levels."

Even with this kind of volatility, people still believe that the stock market is a viable place to invest money for the big payout in the future, as promised by Santa Claus. Here is a March 2009 quote from James Berman on his *Huffington Post* blog:

> It may seem counter-intuitive to make the case for stock investment against such a backdrop, but so much value now resides in so many stocks that there's never been a better time to remain in stocks—or to buy more with bonds or cash. I realize that my words must seem ridiculous, even insulting at this point, given that I said the same thing six months ago when the Dow was down only half as much as it is now. I also realize that the more undervalued stocks get, the less people like investing in them. Call it the investor's paradox. But the case for the value in stocks can only be understood by understanding what a stock really is—a claim on the future cash flows of a business.[8]

I guess we'd better hope that businesses *have* a cash flow in the future. Recent press reports have said that businesses in America are hoarding trillions of dollars in cash—because they are afraid to spend

---

8   James Berman, "Reports of the Death of Equities: Greatly Exaggerated," *Huffington Post*, March 11, 2009, http://www.huffingtonpost.com/james-berman/reports-of-the-death-of-e_b_173460.html.

it, given the uncertain times. I highly recommend that you look up Berman's post at http://www.huffingtonpost.com/james-berman/reports-of-the-death-of-e_b_173460.html to see the excerpt I have used in the context that it came from and read the concise strategy he gives to support his statements.

To me, these "experts" on Wall Street are optimists. Their singing of the "Keep Investing in Wall Street" Christmas carol is starting to get to me. Pavlov's dog lives!

With some recent claims that the recession is over because of the performance of certain stock indices, it really makes me wonder if in fact the "people in the know" are trying to make it look like the stock market is recovering so they can keep meeting their payrolls. If your monthly payroll deduction for investing keeps being invested in stocks, then as long as the market looks like it is performing, no matter how little, there will be a bull market, then a bear market, then bull, then bear, ad nauseum—relatively normal behavior for the stock market—and yet the whole time the bear markets are just a cover for them taking your money out to meet their payrolls. BusinessDictionary.com provides us with these definitions:

> **bull market**: Securities or commodities market in which prices are rising, bulls are trading in high volumes, investment interest is high, and the public views the economy as strong and getting stronger. Some US bull markets (like the one that ended in the year 2000) have lasted for more than 15 years.[9]
>
> **bear market**: Period in which prices of securities or commodities fall by 20 percent or more. During such periods (1) investment interest is generally limited, (2) concerns about the state of the economy abound, and (3) dealers or speculators are more inclined in selling their investment portfolios than to increase their risk by holding.[10]

---

9 *BusinessDictionary.com*, s.v. "bull market," http://www.businessdictionary.com/definition/bull-market.html.
10 *BusinessDictionary.com*, s.v. "bear market," http://www.businessdictionary.com/definition/bear-market.html.

As Investopedia explains it, "A bull thrusts its horns up into the air while a bear swipes its paws down."[11]

When I research *exactly* how investing works, I get theoretical premises that are difficult to understand. If you can make heads or tails of the theory, it turns out that the theory has holes in it like Swiss cheese.

There is an alarming similarity between young children questioning Santa Claus and grown-ups questioning how investing works. We wonder, "Am I going to get concrete answers that will make me feel confident about investing?" Here is a not-so-motivating explanation from BusinessDictionary.com of something called the "greater fool theory":

> Observation that any price (no matter how unrealistic) can be justified if a buyer believes that there is another buyer who will pay an even-higher price for the same item. This line of thinking causes and fuels stockmarket and commodity market booms and manias which, in due course, lead to busts and paranoias.[12]

Should I feel secure knowing that the "experts" on Wall Street are out there investing my money using the "greater fool theory"? Apparently this is the investing tool that led to the great "dot-com" bust of the late '90s.

I think it is important to find these types of irrationalities in practice and match them up to the irrationalities of the Santa Claus theory.

---

11 "Investopedia Explains Bull Market," *Investopedia*, http://www.investopedia.com/terms/b/bullmarket.asp.
12 *BusinessDictionary.com*, s.v. "greater fool theory," http://www.businessdictionary.com/definition/greater-fool-theory.html.

Chapter 4
Manipulation and
Disinformation

The system of banking we have both equally and ever reprobated. I contemplate it as a blot left in all our constitutions, which, if not covered, will end in their destruction, which is already hit by the gamblers in corruption, and is sweeping away in its progress the fortunes and morals of our citizens.

—*Thomas Jefferson, 1802*[13]

So where does all of your money go when the stock market shrinks?

Evidence is starting to emerge that there is a small group of business people who manipulate the stock market through their control of large portions of stock and their influence over fund managers, the Securities and Exchange Commission (or SEC—responsible for monitoring Wall Street), and the media.[14] Through these means, they are able to make millions by pulling money out in ways that are not usually very clear or are cleverly disguised. There is a need to consider the ethics of the fund managers themselves.

The following is an excerpt from an article that appeared in the

---

13   Source: Memoirs, Correspondence, and Private Papers of Thomas Jefferson, vol. 4, Thomas Jefferson Randolph, ed., 1829, pp. 285-288.
14   Deep Capture, http://www.deepcapture.com/.

Huffington Post about a 2006 interview that Jim Cramer, host of CNBC's *Mad Money*, gave to Aaron Task of TheStreet:

> The host of *Mad Money* says he regularly manipulated the market when he ran his hedge fund. He also calls *Wall Street Journal* reporters "bozos" and says behaving illegally is okay because the SEC doesn't understand it anyway.[15]

Manipulating the stock market can be done by just about anyone, from the CEO on down. Here is a quote from a March 11, 2009, *Huffington Post* article by independent writer/producer/director Diane Tucker:

> Whole Foods CEO John Mackey was caught making pseudonymous posts on financial message boards. We could try and imagine how much disinformation is creeping through the Internet, but we'd probably never stop throwing up.[16]

So how much financial disinformation is out there? As Shahien Nasiripour wrote in a *Huffington Post* article from September 25, 2010:

> During a little-noticed hearing this week in Sacramento, Calif., a firm hired by Wall Street to analyze mortgages given to borrowers with poor credit, which were then packaged and sold to investors during the boom years, revealed that as much as 28 percent of those loans failed to meet basic underwriting standards—and Wall Street knew all along.[17]

---

15 Julie Satow, "Jim Cramer Shorting Stocks, Manipulating Markets, Saying the SEC Doesn't Understand," *Huffington Post*, March 11, 2009, http://www.huffingtonpost.com/2009/03/11/jim-cramer-shorting-stock_n_173824.html.
16 Diane Tucker, "The Naked Untruth: Overstock.com CEO Patrick Byrne Hoodwinks DailyKos Diarist," *Huffington Post*, March 11, 2009, http://www.huffingtonpost.com/diane-tucker/the-naked-untruth-ceos-de_b_173754.html.
17 Shahien Nasiripour, "New Proof Wall Street Knew Its Mortgage Securities Were Subpar: Clayton Execs Testify," *Huffington Post*, September 25, 2010, http://

As I said earlier, there are a lot of people who have an interest in keeping you investing your money in the stock market *not* so that you can retire on a nice bed of money but so that they can remove it from under the Christmas tree for their benefit, not yours. To do that, they need you to keep believing in Santa Claus.

It seems that there are, as Jim Cramer said prior, some issues with how effective the SEC regulations are and the ability of the SEC to monitor this. In the largest Ponzi scheme ever seen in this modern time, Bernard Madoff managed to avoid regulators by, as Miles Goslett describes in a *Mail Online* article from January 2009, shouting down any naysayers regarding the validity of the returns on his fund:

> If anyone in the office didn't agree with him or he felt he was being pressurized, he would assert himself by shouting at employees: "It's my bat and my ball!"[18]

How effective was his shouting at people to get them to stop investigating him? Here is a summary from Larry Neumeister and Tom Hays in the *Huffington Post*:

> The fraud, which prosecutors say may have totaled nearly $65 billion, turned a well-respected investment professional—he was once chairman of the Nasdaq exchange—into a symbol of Wall Street greed amid the economic meltdown. The public fury toward him was so great that he was known to wear a bulletproof vest to court. Madoff pleaded guilty to charges including fraud, perjury and money-laundering, telling the judge that the scheme began in the early 1990s, when the country was in a recession and the market was not doing well.[19]

---

www.huffingtonpost.com/2010/09/25/wall-street-subprime-crisis_n_739294.html.

18   Miles Goslett, "I Just Can't Live with That Camera—It's Not Square ... Inside the Bizarre World of £30bn Pyramid Schemester Bernie Madoff," *Mail Online*, January 3, 2009, http://www.dailymail.co.uk/femail/article-1104748/Inside-bizarre-world-30bn-pyramid-schemester-Bernie-Madoff.html.

19   Larry Neumeister and Tom Hays, "Madoff Sent to Jail as Furious Victims

By pleading guilty, Madoff did not have to implicate anyone else. So what can be done to make sure this doesn't happen again? We are all familiar with the effectiveness of the things that White House spokespeople say. From the same *Huffington Post* article by Neumeister and Hays:

> White House spokesman Robert Gibbs said: "The Obama administration will do everything possible to ensure strict enforcement of securities regulations and hope that through those actions that that kind of greed and irresponsibility and that kind of criminal activity never happens again." Investigators are still undertaking the daunting task of unraveling how (Madoff) pulled off the fraud for decades without being caught.[20]

Should I feel secure knowing that the White House version of "everything possible" still may not be enough? Not so much.

Applaud," *Huffington Post*, December 3, 2009, http://www.huffingtonpost.com/2009/03/12/madoff-arrives-in-court-f_n_174194.html.
20 Ibid.

Chapter 5
The Wolves Are Guarding the Henhouse

The name Harry Markopolos may not be a household name, but there are likely many Wall Street traders who now don't sleep well at night knowing he is out there watching. Markopolos is the man who brought down Bernie Madoff. In the March 16, 2009, edition of the *Los Angeles Times*, business analyst Michael Hiltzik wrote of Markopolos's efforts:

> Some of his insights were blazingly simple: In mathematical terms, the split-strike strategy could not have produced the returns Madoff claimed, and in any event would have required option trades amounting to many times the documented trading volume on option markets. Markopolos pleaded with the SEC simply to check his math, to no avail. The agency did place Madoff under oath in 2006, only to blindly accept his brazen lies and forged documents

as the truth. What hasn't been widely reported is that Markopolos also pointed the finger at numerous eminent financial institutions, including Goldman Sachs Group Inc., Morgan Stanley and JPMorgan Chase & Co., suggesting that their option-trading bosses almost certainly knew that Madoff's strategy was a sham. Morgan Stanley and Merrill Lynch reportedly warned some clients not to invest with Madoff.[21]

Some have said of the stock market, "The wolves are guarding the henhouse." In a December 20, 2008, post entitled "The SEC Did Nothing on Madoff," blogger Mathew Gross wrote:

> When the history of this financial meltdown is finally written—and it is not over yet, not by a long shot—central to that story will be the role that the Bush administration's SEC played in allowing criminality to become the modus operandi of Wall Street.
>
> George W. Bush likes to quip that Wall Street got drunk, and we got the hangover. It's a good quip, but let's not forget (to expand the metaphor) that the SEC was the bartender, shouting over the din that the drinks were on the house.[22]

More on the relationship between Madoff and the SEC, and an opinion from one of Madoff's victims, from a March 2009 *Los Angeles Times* article by Walter Hamilton:

> Judith Welling, 71, who with her husband lost about $2.5 million, said Madoff should be sent to

---

21 Michael Hiltzik, "How Could Savvy Investors Have Been Fooled by Madoff? Easy," *Los Angeles Times*, March 16, 2009, http://articles.latimes.com/2009/mar/16/business/fi-hiltzik16.

22 Mathew Gross, "The SEC Did Nothing on Madoff," *Deride and Conquer* (blog), December 20, 2008, http://mathewgross.com/2008/12/the-sec-did-nothing-on-madoff/.

a penitentiary with hardened criminals rather than a more lenient minimum-security prison with other white-collar felons. "As far as I'm concerned, he should go to Rikers [Island]," she said. She also blamed the Securities and Exchange Commission, which missed several opportunities to ferret out Madoff's fraud. Mary L. Schapiro, the new SEC chairwoman, said the agency was beefing up its enforcement and inspection capabilities to prevent a repeat of the Madoff case. "I would never sit here and tell you that I think had we had more resources, the agency would have caught the Madoff fraud earlier on."[23]

And following on the heels of the Madoff embarrassment is the AIG debacle. I love statistics, although my wife says that statistics just clutter my mind. Matt Taibbi came up with the following statistic, as published in *Rolling Stone*:

> In the final three months of last year [2008], (AIG) lost more than $27 million *every hour*. That's $465,000 a minute, a yearly income for a median American household every six seconds, roughly $7,750 a second.[24]

It is interesting when journalists use words like "bets" as if they were covering Texas Hold'em poker tournaments. Here Taibbi continues his *Rolling Stone* article with his take on the AIG debacle from a gambling perspective:

> These same insiders first wrecked the financial world, then cunningly granted themselves nearly unlimited emergency powers to clean up their own mess. And

---

23 Walter Hamilton, "'Sorry' Is Not Enough, Madoff's Victims Say," *Los Angeles Times*, March 13, 2009, http://articles.latimes.com/2009/mar/13/business/fi-madoff13.

24 Matt Taibbi, "The Big Takeover," *Rolling Stone*, March 19, 2009, accessed March 19, 2009, http://www.rollingstone.com/politics/story/26793903/the_big_takeover/print.

so the gambling-addict leaders of companies like AIG end up not penniless and in jail, but with an *Alien*-style death grip on the Treasury and the Federal Reserve—"our partners in the government," as Liddy put it with a shockingly casual matter-of-factness after the most recent bailout.[25]

When there was a brief rally on the stock market on March 12, 2009, the following article by Madlen Read appeared in the *Huffington Post*:

> This week's rally got an extra dose of adrenalin after an accounting board told Congress Thursday it may recommend a let-up in accounting rules for troubled banks in three weeks.[26]

Why would there be a let-up in accounting rules for troubled banks? I thought we were going the other way?!? Didn't we learn any lessons? Who's responsible for monitoring this?

It seems that the SEC is incompetent, but did you know that the securities industry has its own self-policing organization, the Financial Industry Regulatory Authority? Harry Markopolos described this organization as "very corrupt." That organization was once headed by Mary Schapiro, President Barack Obama's new SEC chief. And more about the people in charge, from Pat Garofalo in a 2008 post on *Think Progress*:

> Christopher Cox, Chairman of the Securities and Exchange Commission (SEC), testified that deregulation was a cause of the current financial crisis, including a "regulatory hole" in the credit swap market:
>
> There is another similar regulatory hole that must be

---

25 Ibid.
26 Madlen Read, "Stocks Rally on Good News for Banks, GM, Retailers," *Huffington Post*, March 12, 2009, http://www.huffingtonpost.com/2009/03/12/stocks-mixed-after-jobles_n_174242.html.

immediately addressed to avoid similar consequences. The $58 trillion national market in credit default swaps—double the amount outstanding in 2006—is regulated by no one. Neither the SEC nor any regulator has authority over the CDS market, even to require minimal disclosure to the market.

It's rather ironic that Cox is now calling for regulation of the credit swap market. After all, trading in the credit swap market was what sunk insurance giant AIG. Once AIG had "sold large quantities of credit-default swaps to financial institutions around the world," it required an $85 billion federal bailout to keep its failure from affecting the wider financial system ...

The Bush administration found the credit crisis so manageable that it "unveiled a widely discussed blueprint for U.S. financial regulatory reform that called for less supervision of Wall Street by the Securities and Exchange Commission." Cox has now realized that a lack of "regulatory authority" is a "mistake," but only after seeing the result years of deregulation has had on the financial system.[27]

Are you feeling more confident about your belief in Santa? Do you feel like putting your money under the Christmas tree? A February 2009 article in the Independent notes that:

... even Alan Greenspan, high priest of laissez-faire [and former chairman of the US Federal Reserve], has said he was mistaken to believe investors could be trusted to rein in risky practices. Now we see it even more clearly with Madoff: everyone seemed to be trusting to everyone else to do the due diligence that

---

27 Pat Garofalo, "SEC Chairman Christopher Cox Finally Realizes the Problem With Deregulation," *The Wonk Room* (blog), *Think Progress*, September 24, 2008, http://wonkroom.thinkprogress.org/2008/09/24/cox-deregulation/.

should have been their own responsibility, even the wise men and the superwomen. A new era of harsher regulation is just around the corner. Wall Street, it seems, simply cannot be trusted.[28]

Here is a note on what the American government does and does not look for, from Matt Taibbi in *Rolling Stone*, with reference to the AIG debacle:

> And all this happened at the end of eight straight years that America devoted to frantically chasing the shadow of a terrorist threat to no avail; eight years spent stopping every citizen at every airport to search every purse, bag, crotch and briefcase for juice boxes and explosive tubes of toothpaste. Yet in the end, our government had no mechanism for searching the balance sheets of companies that held life-or-death power over our society and was unable to spot holes in the national economy the size of Libya (whose entire GDP last year was smaller than AIG's 2008 losses).[29]

And what about the people who caused this mess in the first place? How are they doing? In the *Los Angeles Times* article mentioned at the start of this chapter, Michael Hiltzik goes on to say:

> The latest development in the mortgage market fomenting outrage in the streets and condemnation across the media spectrum is the spectacle of rich investors—Wall Street traders, hedge fund operators, even former executives of the detested Countrywide Financial Corp.—buying up delinquent home loans, reworking terms for borrowers, and selling them off

---

28 "The Madoff Files: Bernie's Billions," *Independent*, January 29, 2009, http://www.independent.co.uk/news/business/analysis-and-features/the-madoff-files-bernies-billions-1518939.html.
29 Matt Taibbi, "The Big Takeover," *Rolling Stone*, March 19, 2009, accessed March 19, 2009, http://www.rollingstone.com/politics/story/26793903/the_big_takeover/print.

to new investors at a handsome profit. Here's what I think about these bottom feeders: God bless them.

He implies that this is a fantastic outcome now that rich investors, who may have had a hand in the financial crisis in the first place, can get even richer by doing what the banks were supposed to do. In summary, we have "experts" on Wall Street committing legal "frauds" of gargantuan proportions; a regulatory agency that is incompetent; banks that cannot do their job; and a fair amount of panic as to how to fix the problems. Now *that* is a recipe to make me *not* want to believe in Santa Claus and inspire me to take all of my money *out* from under the Christmas tree.

Chapter 6
Fixing the Mess

It seems that no one can agree on how to fix the problem. There are those who believe that the government bailouts are exactly the wrong thing to do.

The US risks sending the world into a depression as its bailouts of failed companies rob healthy businesses of capital, investor Jim Rogers said in a Bloomberg interview.[30]

The US government should let American International Group Inc., whose fourth-quarter loss was the worst in corporate history, go bankrupt, Rogers added.

Like teaching a child to ride a bike, sometimes you just have to let them fall. Here is an excerpt from a February 1, 2009, *CNN World* interview with Peter Schiff. Here Schiff discusses the benefits of letting large corporations like General Motors fail:

> **Host**: So what would the solution be according to you? Just let companies that are in trouble fail?
>
> **Peter Schiff**: Absolutely.
>
> **Host**: But look at the auto industry. You're looking at

---
30 Chua Kong Ho and Bernard Lo, "U.S. Bailouts Add to Risk of Depression, Rogers Says (Update2)," *Bloomberg*, March 17, 2009, http://www.bloomberg.com/apps/news?pid=20601087&sid=a3kTp0KUJWWE&refer=worldwide.

millions of people who depend on that industry. That would be a catastrophe.

Peter Schiff: But just turning it over to government control is not going to make their jobs safer. What we need is a vibrant, competitive automobile industry, and we're not going to get one if we support the status quo. We need to let the market work. We need to let the companies go through bankruptcy. We need to let management be changed ... You don't want to make the false conclusion that just because we support these jobs that the economy is going to prosper. You're going to destroy other jobs that you can't measure. And in the long run, the cost of bailing out companies like General Motors is worse than the cost of letting them fail. It's always better to let the market function.[31]

It seems simple enough in an ideal world—businesses get started in America, hire Americans to do the work, and the goods get bought by Americans. And if there is excess capacity, maybe we can export some of our goods, too. If a company fails, it goes bankrupt, and the market will recover. But again, we just can't seem to agree. From *MarketWatch*, March 19, 2009:

> The Federal Reserve's decision Wednesday to buy $300 billion in longer-term Treasury securities has ignited a firestorm, with analysts saying it will either cause a currency crisis or jolt the economy out of the morgue.
>
> "We're in a car heading for a cliff and the Fed has just stepped on the gas," said Peter Schiff ... one of a handful of economists who worried about the economy long before it slipped into a severe recession.
>
> On the other hand, David Jones, chief executive of

---

31 Peter Schiff, interview on *CNN World*, CNN, February 1, 2009, http://www.youtube.com/watch?v=CXLgVJhVqPw.

DMJ Advisors and a long-time Fed watcher, hailed Bernanke's decision as a "turning point" for the economy.

The Fed's plan now is essentially to print money to raise the supply of credit …

Schiff believes that the move will lead to a collapse of the value of the dollar, an outcome he has long predicted.[32]

As with any good screw-up, we just can't agree on how to fix it. But how do you convince people to start buying again? And I don't mean on credit. Credit is what got us into this mess in the first place.

It was only recently that I discovered one of the amazing ways that people get themselves into debt—and of all things, it is through investing. My life-insurance agent retired recently, and his replacement turned out to be a certified financial planner. So our new agent phoned up and asked if he could come by to discuss our situation. He told us that the smart thing to do was to borrow $100,000 and invest it. This way we could write off the "carrying charges" (interest) that would take the place of the tax break that would be achieved through 401K or RRSP donations. Then I was to give the $100,000 to him, and he would invest it and make great rewards for me.

He gave us several examples of how this had worked so well for his clients and even himself. We turned down his offer but were amazed at the idea that the benefits outweighed the risk. I had always heard that people who invest successfully never use their own money. But is this how it is possible that, when the stock market tanks, people now find themselves in deep over their heads not able to pay back their loans? This method of investing may have worked well during the heady days (he gave examples of 40 percent gains), but is it still viable? Can Santa Claus deliver that many toys to all of the risk-taking adventurers around the world?

---

32 Greg Robb, "Fed Crosses Rubicon and Sets Off Firestorm," *MarketWatch*, March 19, 2009, http://www.marketwatch.com/news/story/Fed-crosses-rubicon-setting-off/story.aspx?guid={CC678D54-22B8-4E39-8F0B-13A24308E7E8}.

Chapter 7
Give Us Our Jobs Back

To get people to start spending again, in my humble, uneducated opinion, we just need to give them their jobs back. Unfortunately, that may not be possible. So how about, at the very least, giving them jobs—jobs that pay a sustainable wage. Or did we outsource all of those types of jobs?

Seldom, if ever, do I hear the "experts" on Wall Street say that we need to give jobs back to the people. From the *New York Times*, August 1, 2009:

> Over the coming months, as many as 1.5 million jobless Americans will exhaust their unemployment insurance benefits, ending what for some has been a last bulwark against foreclosures and destitution. Because of emergency extensions already enacted by Congress, laid-off workers in nearly half the states can collect benefits for up to 79 weeks, the longest period since the unemployment insurance program was created in the 1930s. But unemployment in this

recession has proved to be especially tenacious, and a wave of job-seekers is using up even this prolonged aid. Tens of thousands of workers have already used up their benefits, and the numbers are expected to soar in the months to come, reaching half a million by the end of September and 1.5 million by the end of the year, according to new projections by the National Employment Law Project, a private research group. Unemployment insurance is now a lifeline for nine million Americans, with payments averaging just over $300 per week.[33]

Here is another excerpt from the *CNN World* interview with Peter Schiff, February 1, 2009. Peter's point here is that there is a misunderstanding around how the people trying to solve the problem are unaware that unemployment is a major factor in the recession crisis:

> I think the unemployment problem is already greater than they realize. I think there's a lot of people who have left the workforce; they're discards; they're not being counted. There's a lot of people who are working part-time who would rather be working full-time. I think there are a lot of independent contractors and a lot of commissioned salespeople who are still employed, but they're barely making any money.[34]

And following along on my motto that "it can always get worse" is a June 22, 2009, excerpt from Michael Fletcher of the *Washington Post*:

> With many forecasters projecting unemployment to remain above 10 percent next year and not return

---

33 Erik Eckholm, "Prolonged Aid to Unemployed Is Running Out," *New York Times*, August 1, 2009, http://www.nytimes.com/2009/08/02/us/02unemploy.html.

34 Peter Schiff, interview on *CNN World*, CNN, February 1, 2009, http://www.youtube.com/watch?v=CXLgVJhVqPw.

to pre-recession levels of roughly 5 percent for years after that, Obama is likely to be confronted with defending the effectiveness of his economic policies as the nation endures its worst employment situation in a generation. Analysts say the high levels of joblessness would be accompanied by increases in child poverty, strained government budgets, and Black and Latino unemployment rates approaching 20 percent.

"I find it unfathomable that people are not horrified about what is going to happen," said Lawrence Mishel, president of the Economic Policy Institute. "I regard all this talk about how the recession is maybe going to end, all the talk about deficits and inflation, to be the equivalent of telling Americans, 'You are just going to have to tough it out.' But we're looking at persistent unemployment that is going to be extraordinarily damaging to many communities."[35]

Mishel's one line here sums it up in a nutshell: "I find it unfathomable that people are not horrified about what is going to happen ..." I guess it's kind of like watching a train wreck. What kind of pain might it wreak? In a July 2009 *Washington Post* article, Louis Gill, the director of the Bakersfield Homeless Center in California, said, "Last year, we saw a 34 percent increase in homeless families and a 24 percent increase in homeless children." The article continues:

> The stereotype of a homeless person as a single man no longer applies. A resident of the Bakersfield center is far more likely to be a young mother with a "good, solid job and a mortgage that she just couldn't pay." The ravages of the recession, including a surge in foreclosures and unemployment approaching 10 percent, have driven thousands of families onto the streets.... The number of homeless families rose 9

---

35 Michael A. Fletcher, "Recovery's Missing Ingredient: New Jobs," *Washington Post*, June 22, 2009, http://www.washingtonpost.com/wp-dyn/content/article/2009/06/21.

percent, and in rural and suburban areas the number jumped by 56 percent.³⁶

Let's remember that on July 12, 2009, President Barak Obama had this to say:

> We took steps to restart lending to families and businesses, stabilize our major financial institutions, and help homeowners stay in their homes and pay their mortgages.³⁷

But in a September 23, 2010, *Huffington Post* interview, Al Franken, Democratic senator for Minnesota, pointed out:

> "Millions of families are losing their homes in the current housing crisis so I'm outraged when I hear stories that show how broken the mortgage services industry is … The actions of Ally Financial are just another example of why we need to strengthen the Home Affordable Modification Program."
>
> Ally Financial, the nation's fourth-largest home lender, halted evictions in 23 states this week after it was revealed that a document processor signed off on thousands … of foreclosure documents every week without verifying any of the information in the paperwork.³⁸

---

36 Alexi Mostrous, "More Families Are Becoming Homeless; Largest Increases in 2008 Came in Rural and Suburban Areas, Study Finds," *Washington Post*, July 12, 2009, accessed July 12, 2009, http://www.washingtonpost.com/wp-dyn/content/article/2009/07/11.

37 Barak Obama, "Building Something Better," *Washington Post*, July 12, 2009, http://www.washingtonpost.com/wp-dyn/content/article/2009/07/11/AR2009071100647.html.

38 Arthur Delaney, "Al Franken: Foreclosure Paperwork Scandal Shows Need to Strengthen HAMP," *Huffington Post*, September 23, 2010, http://www.huffingtonpost.com/2010/09/23/bogus-affidavits-in-gmac-_n_734742.html.

One day after that quote was published, *Huffington Post* writer Arthur Delaney followed up with this article:

> Congressional Democrats want to know why government-backed mortgage finance giant Fannie Mae is farming out foreclosure paperwork to "foreclosure mill" law firms accused of rubber-stamping tens of thousands of possibly bogus documents.
>
> "The firms have been accused of fabricating or backdating documents, as well as lying to conceal the true owner of a note," wrote House Financial Services Committee chairman Barney Frank, Rep. Alan Grayson, and Rep. Corrine Brown in a letter to Fannie Mae president Michael Williams. "Why is Fannie Mae using lawyers that are accused of regularly engaging in fraud to kick people out of their homes?" wrote Frank et al in their letter.[39]

And now, in the fall of 2010, the end of the New Deal–style program is upon us. This program saw a billion dollars go to pay salaries of people so they could keep their jobs in governments, NGOs, and small businesses. If the program is not renewed, tens of thousands of people will lose their jobs.[40]

Unemployment is not the only fear. The adjunct to unemployment is the *threat* of losing one's current job. As the reality of the depth of this financial crisis keeps getting worse, despite the best efforts by the "experts" on Wall Street to say that it will end "soon," people are holding on to what little money they have. In a last ditch effort to save their homes, some will drain their savings and run up their credit-card debt, while some will (and do) find it better to just walk away from their now devalued homes—that is, in the states that will allow you

---

[39] Arthur Delaney, "Dems to Fannie Mae: Why Are You Feeding Foreclosure Mills?" *Huffington Post*, September 24, 2010, http://www.huffingtonpost.com/2010/09/24/house-democrats-to-fannie_n_738280.html.

[40] Michael Cooper, "Job Loss Looms as Part of Stimulus Act Expires," *New York Times*, September 25, 2010, http://www.nytimes.com/2010/09/26/us/26stimulus.html.

to walk away, versus the states that allow the banks to hunt you down to get their due.

In a *New York Times* interview from May 2009, an Obama adviser offers an interesting opinion on when this recession might hit bottom:

> Robert Reich, who served as labor secretary under President Bill Clinton and advised the Obama campaign, said on Sunday that the rate of growth would have to be higher—4.5 percent—to reverse rising unemployment.
>
> "I think that when we talk about—or anybody talks about—hitting bottom, what we really have to understand is that the bottom is a kind of an undefined concept here," he said on ABC's "This Week."[41]

Can the $800 billion stimulus program solve the unemployment problem? Senator Eric Cantor weighs in with his thoughts at the end of this excerpt from a July 2009 *Washington Post* article:

> Leading economists agree that the most powerful effects of the stimulus package have yet to be felt … It would barely offset the 433,000 jobs the nation lost last month alone, and the resulting employment would represent a drop in the bucket compared with the 6.5 million jobs lost since the recession began in December 2007 …
>
> Noting that the Obama administration predicted earlier this year that stimulus spending would keep the unemployment rate under 8 percent, Rep. Eric Cantor (R-Va.), the No. 2 Republican in the House, said, "… any objective measure would indicate there's a failure when you have a commitment of nearly $800

---

41 Joshua Brustein, "Obama Adviser Sees Unemployment Rising Until 2010," *New York Times*, May 10, 2009, http://www.nytimes.com/2009/05/11/business/economy/11jobs.html.

billion in taxpayer funds and have the type of job loss we're experiencing."[42]

How could we end our economic crisis? Here's my answer: Create jobs for people that pay a living wage. Give people job security. If people have jobs, with job security, they will start to spend again. Unions understood this years ago.

So how do we create jobs? Dan Froomkin, senior Washington correspondent for the *Huffington Post*, has a series on ways to create jobs. I am not here to weigh in on the merits and drawbacks of each suggestion, but at least someone is thinking, and I encourage you to go to his posts and read the full articles for yourself. Some of the suggestions he's written about:

- A temporary stoppage of the payroll tax.[43]
- A New Deal–style program that would see the feds share revenue with the states to create or maintain jobs.[44]
- A massive investment in retrofitting buildings to make them more energy efficient.[45]
- An enormous investment in green technology and green jobs.[46]

---

42 Lori Montgomery, "Power of Stimulus Slow to Take Hold," *Washington Post*, July 8, 2009, http://www.washingtonpost.com/wp-dyn/content/article/2009/07/07.
43 Dan Froomkin, "'America Needs Jobs' Idea No. 1: A Payroll Tax Holiday," *Huffington Post*, September 21, 2010, http://www.huffingtonpost.com/2010/09/21/payroll-tax-holiday_n_732179.html.
44 Dan Froomkin, "Job-Creation Idea No. 2: Rescue The States," *Huffington Post*, September 22, 2010, http://www.huffingtonpost.com/2010/09/22/jobcreation-idea-no-2-res_n_734460.html; Steven T. Goldberg, "Robert Shiller Suggests a New Deal-Style Solution to Unemployment," *Kiplinger*, September 21, 2010, http://www.kiplinger.com/columns/value/archive/robert-shiller-suggests-a-new-deal-style-solution-unemployment.html.
45 Dan Froomkin, "Job-Creation Idea No. 3: The Joys of Retrofitting," *Huffington Post*, September 23, 2010, http://www.huffingtonpost.com/2010/09/23/jobcreation-idea-no-3-the_n_736271.html.
46 Dan Froomkin, "A Convenient Truth: Gearing Up for Climate Change Could Supercharge the Job Market," *Huffington Post*, September 28, 2010, http://www.huffingtonpost.com/2010/09/28/a-convenient-truth-gearin_n_741430.html.

- "Rather than lay off a portion of their work force, employers would reduce the hours of [their] workers. And a special Unemployment Insurance program would make up some or all of the workers' lost income."[47]
- "Rolling back a 2004 law the Bush administration pushed through Congress, which barred an estimated six million workers from receiving overtime pay." Then increase overtime pay to triple time to give corporations an incentive to hire more workers.[48]
- "Get tougher on China, threatening to impose tariffs unless it stops manipulating its currency … Chinese products and labor would suddenly become much more expensive. The ensuing shift in cost-benefit analyses would likely generate hundreds of thousands of American jobs."[49]
- "Do what Franklin Delano Roosevelt did during the great Depression … directly employ millions of Americans, most notably through the Works Progress Administration (WPA) and the Civilian Conservation Corps (CCC) … men and women who planted trees, constructed state parks, created great works of art and built bridges, dams and other structure."[50]
- Encourage banks to lend.[51]

---

47 Dan Froomkin, "Sharing the Pain of Layoffs Means Losing Fewer Jobs," *Huffington Post*, September 29, 2010, http://www.huffingtonpost.com/2010/09/29/work-sharing-layoffs_n_744302.html.
48 Dan Froomkin, "Sharing the Pain of Layoffs Means Losing Fewer Jobs," *Huffington Post*, September 29, 2010, http://www.huffingtonpost.com/2010/09/29/work-sharing-layoffs_n_744302.html.
49 Dan Froomkin, "Job-Creation Idea No. 7: Drawing a Line with China," *Huffington Post*, October 1, 2010, http://www.huffingtonpost.com/2010/10/01/drawing-a-line-with-china_n_746596.html.
50 Dan Froomkin, "Job Creation Idea No. 8: Time for a New WPA," *Huffington Post*, October 8, 2010, http://www.huffingtonpost.com/2010/10/08/america-needs-jobs-time-f_n_754859.html.
51 Dan Froomkin, "Job-Creation Idea No. 9: Encourage Banks to Lend—Or Else," *Huffington Post*, October 12, 2010, http://www.huffingtonpost.com/2010/10/12/job-creation-idea-no-9-en_n_759329.html.

- "A lower dollar would level the playing field.... As long as the dollar remains high, it acts like an enormous tax on U.S. exports and a massive subsidy for U.S. imports."[52]
- Buy from manufacturers who manufacture within your borders.[53]
- "Lower the retirement age ... a three-year window during which workers aged 62 and older could retire on full Social Security."[54]
- Build infrastructure to create jobs and increase productivity.[55]

When I was explaining the premise of this book to a friend, his first criticism of my philosophy was, "Well, it's very difficult to create jobs."

I know I am preaching to the choir when I say that if we hadn't sent all of those jobs to other countries, we might be in a much better position to be employing more people today. And for Christ's sake, buy something local or domestic, not foreign or imported! Yes, I know, we all fail at this one. I drive a Japanese-made Honda, but my guitar is an American-made Gibson!

Here is one job-creation success story, albeit small, that involves using current stimulus money in a New Deal–style program:

> After the Armstrong Pie Company hired 12 workers with stimulus money, it was able to expand its production, add delivery routes and increase sales, said Dalyn Patterson, who owns the company with

---

52 Dan Froomkin, "Job-Creation Idea No. 10: A Lower Dollar Would Level the Playing Field," *Huffington Post*, October 15, 2010, http://www.huffingtonpost.com/2010/10/15/jobcreation-idea-no-10-a-_n_763862.html.
53 Dan Froomkin, "Job-Creation Idea No. 11: Buy American—If You Can," *Huffington Post*, October 25, 2010, http://www.huffingtonpost.com/2010/10/21/buy-american_n_771211.html.
54 Dan Froomkin, "Job-Creation Idea No. 12: Let the Old Folks Retire Early and Make Way for Young Workers," *Huffington Post*, October 25, 2010, http://www.huffingtonpost.com/2010/10/25/jobcreation-idea-no-12-le_n_773391.html.
55 Dan Froomkin, "Job-Creation Idea No. 13: No Better Time than Now to Build the Future," *Huffington Post*, October 28, 2010, http://www.huffingtonpost.com/2010/10/28/jobcreation-idea-no-13-no_n_775265.html.

her husband, Bert. The business increased enough that she said she expected to keep 11 of the 12 workers.[56]

Critics will argue that this is tantamount to socialism, but the critics of socialism seem willing to ignore the socialist bailouts of the airline industry after the events of September 2001 and the socialist bailouts of the auto industry and the banking industry due to our current recession. These right-wing capitalist critics are now reaping the rewards of dividends again from those industries without giving the proper thanks to the socialist government that bailed them out.

What if—and this is a big "what if"—laws were passed that changed the way employers were allowed to lay off? For example, when a company like General Motors closes its plants in Flint, Michigan, or DHL closes its major hub in Wilmington, Ohio, these closures have a deep impact on the community. It's not like those thousands of people are just going to walk down the street to another employer and get another good paying job.

Another issue to consider is the large layoffs that occur when two companies merge. It seems odd that mergers fall under scrutiny for competitiveness laws, but seldom will the courts consider what that merger will do to the employees and the communities, especially in cases where the layoffs will be large due to the merger.

So when is the financial crisis going to end? Here's one opinion from a September 2008 *Wall Street Journal* article:

> Expectations for a quick end to the crisis are fading fast. "I think it's going to last a lot longer than perhaps we would have anticipated," Anne Mulcahy, chief executive of Xerox Corp., said Wednesday.[57]

This next quote from a February 2009 Reuters report seems to be a bit more harsh:

---

56 Michael Cooper, "Job Loss Looms as Part of Stimulus Act Expires," *New York Times*, September 25, 2010, http://www.nytimes.com/2010/09/26/us/26stimulus.html.

57 Jon Hilsenrath, Serena Ng, and Damian Paletta, "Worst Crisis Since '30s, With No End Yet in Sight," *Wall Street Journal*, September 18, 2008, http://online.wsj.com/article/SB122169431617549947.html.

> Investor George Soros said on Friday the world financial system has effectively disintegrated, adding that there is yet no prospect of a near-term resolution to the crisis.[58]

In my humble opinion, the crisis will not end until we solve unemployment.

And how did we get here? During a June 2009 discussion by the editors of the *New York Review of Books*, Bill Bradley had this to say regarding the three biggest mistakes that were made with regard to financial regulation:

> In 1999, we allowed investment banks, banks, insurance companies to combine: we eliminated the Glass-Steagall Act, which prohibited commercial banks from operating as investment banks.
>
> The second mistake was in 1999, the explicit decision by the Clinton administration and Congress not to regulate derivatives, in particular credit default swaps.
>
> The third decision was in 2004. The SEC allowed banks to go from 10 to 1 leverage to 30 to 1 leverage *[Canadian banks were not allowed this increase in leverage, and therefore did not experience the volatility seen by the American banking system]*. Finally, we might want to remember that the chairman of the Federal Reserve is supposed to remove the punch bowl from the party when the party gets out of control.[59]

We want to assume that those in charge at the White House have some control over these things. But it seems apparent that an actual

---

58 Pedro Nicolaci da Costa and Juan Lagorio, "Soros Sees No Bottom for World Financial 'Collapse,'" *Reuters*, February 21, 2009, http://www.reuters.com/article/businessNews/idUSTRE51K0A920090221.
59 Bill Bradley, "The Crisis and How to Deal with It," *New York Review of Books*, June 11, 2009, http://www.nybooks.com/articles/22756.

president does not do all of the research but listens to advisers on certain subjects, especially subjects he doesn't fully understand. Here is President Bill Clinton, as quoted in an April 2010 ABC News blog, weighing in on his contribution to how we got to where we are:

> "On derivatives, yeah I think they were wrong and I think I was wrong to take [their advice] because the argument on derivatives was that these things are expensive and sophisticated and only a handful of investors will buy them and they don't need any extra protection, and any extra transparency ... And the flaw in that argument," Clinton added, "was that first of all sometimes people with a lot of money make stupid decisions and make it without transparency."
>
> The former President also said he was also wrong about understanding the consequences if the derivatives market tanked. "The most important flaw was even if less than 1 percent of the total investment community is involved in derivative exchanges, so much money was involved that if they went bad, they could affect a 100 percent of the investments, and indeed a 100 percent of the citizens in countries, not investors, and I was wrong about that."[60]

Yes, a large majority can be ravaged by a miniscule minority.

---

60 Jake Tapper, "Clinton: I Was Wrong to Listen to Wrong Advice Against Regulating Derivatives," *Political Punch* (blog), ABC News, April 17, 2010, http://blogs.abcnews.com/politicalpunch/2010/04/. Used with permission of ABC News Program Copyright © 2010. All rights reserved.

Chapter 8
Cost Cutting

> Pfizer stock has lost 34 percent of its value since Kindler took over, compared with a drop of 20 percent for the Dow Jones Wilshire Pharmaceuticals Index. Scott Richter, a portfolio manager at Fifth Third Asset Management, dumped his Pfizer shares more than a year ago because the R&D wasn't performing. "Cost-cutting can help earnings in the short term, but it's not transformational," Richter says.[61]
>
> —*Walter Armstrong, "Attack of the Monster Merger"*

I used to work for Wyeth Pharmaceuticals in Collegeville, Pennsylvania (for the geographically challenged, that's just a few miles north of Philadelphia, but it seems longer in traffic). In July of 2002, Wyeth's stock plummeted about 50 percent after the release of a finding by the FDA that studies showed hormone therapy (Wyeth's billion-dollar drug) increased the risk of breast cancer in women.

Inevitably, or so it seemed, four months later the first round of layoffs occurred at Wyeth. Ironically, the first department to get downsized was

---

61 Walter Armstrong, "Attack of the Monster Merger," *Advanstar Communications Inc.*, March 1, 2009, http://pharmexec.findpharma.com/pharmexec/article/articleDetail.jsp?id=585590&pageID=1&sk=&date=. © 2009 Advanstar Communications Inc. All rights reserved.

human resources (HR). The layoff happened on a Monday morning, which is, by tradition, also orientation day for new hires. Orientation day is run by the HR department. So while HR was being downsized, classrooms full of new hires sat waiting for someone to show up to give the orientation. After about two hours, someone (who still had a job in HR) realized that the company had overlooked this logistic, and so deployed sentries to tell the new hires to just go report to their new bosses; the orientation would take place at some other time.

Over the course of the week, many other departments were downsized, including one member of our department.

There are many reasons for downsizing and layoffs. We all know that computers and automation have allowed corporations to use machines to do the work of humans, although the same can be said of washing machines and dishwashers. As Peter Joseph points out in his film *Zeitgeist: Addendum*:

> If we look back at history, we see a very clear pattern of machine automation slowly replacing human labor. From the disappearance of the elevator man to the nearly full automation of an automobile production plant, the fact is, as technology grows, the need for humans in the workforce will continually be diminished. This creates a serious clash, which proves the falseness of the monetary-based labor system, for human employment is in direct competition with technological development. Therefore, given the fundamental priority of profit by industry, people through time will be continually laid off and replaced by machines.[62]

It's interesting to think that the type of university graduate corporations are looking for is the one who can design a process or system that would eliminate the replacement or hiring of anyone— especially university graduates.

And we all know the mantra: keep up with the times and modernization or you won't be competitive. Logically, this does make

---

62 Peter Joseph, *Zeitgeist: Addendum* (GMP, 2008), 2:03:07, http://vimeo.com/13770061.

sense. Obviously, there are times when it is appropriate for modernization to lead a company to a smaller workforce.

In 1952, Kurt Vonnegut wrote a chilling prediction of our current crisis situation in his book called *Player Piano*.[63] It's not a love story. I highly recommend it.

There seem to be times, though, when job layoffs serve other purposes. It seems that sometimes, layoffs are the way companies react to the scolding they get from Wall Street and the business press. How much influence does Wall Street and the press have over the CEOs who run our corporations? In 2009, when Pfizer announced plans to acquire Wyeth as a strategic move to bolster research and development and add more to its portfolio of blockbuster drugs that were not near patent expiry, here is how the press and Wall Street reacted, as reported by Walter Armstrong on PharmExec.com:

> What will Pfizer do? That question has been asked almost daily by Wall Street and the business media since late 2006 ... The No. 1 pharmaceutical company with the best-selling drug in history—and the steepest patent cliff—has come to symbolize the "crisis" of the drug industry and its bankrupt blockbuster model.
>
> News of the deal—the third largest in pharma history—got immediate reviews from Wall Street all the way to Capitol Hill.
>
> The headlines tell the tale: "Not What the Doctor Ordered" in the *Washington Post*. "Pfizer: Try, Try Again" in the *Hartford Courant*.
>
> "Wyeth's Deal Big, But Pfizer Still Needs a Blockbuster" on http://TheStreet.com/.
>
> "Did Pfizer Just Commit Suicide?" on http://MotleyFool.com/.

---

63 Kurt Vonnegut, *Player Piano* (Charles Scribner's Sons, 1952).

"Is Jeffrey Kindler Brave or Crazy?" on the Harvard Business School Web site.

Not all were nasty. Analysts who had long promoted a major merger as Pfizer's only option—the firm had more than $27 billion in cash on its balance sheet at year's end—grudgingly approved. "Pfizer is in the most desperate state of anyone in the industry in terms of patent expirations," says Standard & Poor's analyst Herman Saftlas. "We feel that it is in the best interests of Pfizer to do a deal like this in order to shore up the top line."

Investors voiced their enthusiasm for the deal by sending the company's stock down 10 percent.[64]

There is a standard business practice by which companies forecast expected sales for a period of time, such as the next fiscal quarter or next fiscal year, and that is followed up at the end of said time period by Wall Street either blessing the company when targets are met by increasing the stock price or punishing the company when targets are not met by significantly lowering the stock price. This is also when the company or corporation pays dividends to its investors.

A dividend is merely a return on your investment, the payback for being an investor. It might only be a fifty-cent dividend, but if you own 500,000 shares, that turns into a tidy sum of $250,000. For unlucky investors like me, I have nine shares in Bell Canada, which pays me a quarterly dividend of about $2.44.

If a company had forecast a dividend of eighty cents, but at quarterly dividend time found itself only able to pay fifty cents, this would outrage Wall Street and investors.

This practice, in my uneducated mind, has become the Achilles' heel[65] of capitalist society. There must be many a CEO who does not

---

64 Walter Armstrong, "Attack of the Monster Merger," *PharmaExec.com*, March 1, 2009, http://pharmexec.findpharma.com/pharmexec/article/articleDetail.jsp?id =585590&pageID=1&sk=&date=. © 2009 Advanstar Communications Inc. All rights reserved.

65 "Achilles was the son of Thetis and Peleus, the bravest hero in the Trojan war, according to Greek mythology. When Achilles was born, his mother, Thetis, tried

sleep well the night before earnings are announced. If the target has been missed, Wall Street can make the stock spiral downward, cutting the net value of the company and, at a micro level, making the stocks and stock options that the CEO holds worth much less. I would be remiss if I didn't mention that it makes *everybody's* stocks and stock options worth less, but there is a significant point here with reference to the CEO's own personal stocks.

> *"The love of money is the root of all evil."*
> —Paul the Apostle in his letter to Timothy: 1 Timothy 6:10

No one likes to see millions of dollars go down the drain. I got upset when my bank screwed me around and cost me $300 in interest penalties. So imagine the feeling when you watch $100,000,000 of your money go down the drain.

We could start to suspect that a CEO would take action to prevent having to watch his or her $100,000,000 go down the drain. By the way, the $100,000,000 figure is purely hypothetical, but it looks good to write it out. For some CEOs, the figure could be substantially higher. John Roth, former CEO of Nortel, makes a good example. According to a post by Mark Evans on All About Nortel:

> In the wake of Nortel's plan to settle its outstanding class-action lawsuits with a $2.5-billion stock and cash payment, where does this leave ex-CEO John Roth? One of the lawsuits dates back to activities between 2000 and 2001—during which Roth was CEO. At the time, Roth was going around telling investors that Nortel's 2001 sales would grow by more than 30% and it would take market share from rivals. A month later—surprise, surprise—the bottom falls out of the market, which surprised Nortel despite the

---

to make him immortal by dipping him in the river Styx. As she immersed him, she held him by one heel and forgot to dip him a second time so the heel she held could get wet too. Therefore, the place where she held him remained untouched by the magic water of the Styx and that part stayed mortal or vulnerable. To this day, any weak point is called an 'Achilles' heel.'" http://www.wordinfo.info/words/index/info/view_unit/3648.

fact it had thousands of sales people in the field who could easily get a sense of what customers planned to do. As we all know, Roth conveniently retired in 2001 with $135-million in cash (much of it due to exercising inexpensive options). These days, he's lying low at his estate in Caledon, Ont. with his collection of cars and investment portfolio that does not include Nortel stock (he sold it a year or so ago after lamenting it pained him to see Nortel doing so poorly). For investors wondering if Roth will get away scott-free, there is a class-action lawsuit still outstanding that was filed against Roth and more than two dozen executives and board members.[66]

Yes, it seems that Roth exercised his stock options just before the announcement that the company had missed its targets. Some might view this as "insider trading." From the CBC in Canada:

> When people talk about insider trading, it's usually the illegal variety they're talking about. Illegal insider trading is one of those crimes that drive small investors to distraction. The average retail investor never hears about a coming merger or acquisition before it's publicly announced. They never know of a big new contract or a sudden earnings shortfall before it's splashed all over the business pages ... Unfortunately, some corporate insiders have used their knowledge of non-public key corporate events to profit from developments that only a privileged few are party to. When that happens, the integrity of the market is compromised.[67]

Though, as the article explains, not all insider trading is illegal:

> Company executives frequently buy and sell stock in

---

66 Mark Evans, "Is John Roth Home and Free?" *All About Nortel*, February 11, 2006, http://www.allaboutnortel.com/2006/02/11/is-john-roth-home-and-free/.
67 "Insider Trading—What's the Problem?" CBC Online, December 21, 2005, http://www.cbc.ca/news/background/crime/insider_trading.html.

their own firms. Stock options and grants are a popular way to compensate senior officers in a company. The thinking in many company boardrooms is that there is no better way to ensure that the firm prospers and the stock price rises than to give the people who run it a financial stake in how they perform. Many companies also require their senior officers to own stock in the company equal to as much as six times their annual salary. As long as they report their trades to regulators within 10 days of the trade (and they're not acting on information that has not been publicly disclosed), there's no problem. It's when they act on non-public information that the trade can become illegal.[68]

Okay, so besides the possibility of a CEO doing something illegal, what legal options are available to them to try to meet the target, the forecasted earnings? The simple answer is cost cutting, which comes in many differing forms. Cost cutting can be as simple as reducing the number of olives in the salad:

> American Airlines saved $40,000 in 1987 by eliminating one olive from each salad served in first class. Northwest Airlines has removed children's meals from its US domestic flights in a move to cut costs, as the airline faces increasing pressures due to the economic downturn.[69]

Effective cost cutting can be achieved through such practices as renegotiating with suppliers with regard to their pricing; preferred supplier status; finding new suppliers; and using cheaper supplies for such items as paper, pens, paper clips, and toilet paper (watch out for that cheap toilet paper!).

But these cost-cutting measures are child's play in comparison to the big boys' methods, such as outsourcing and layoffs. Layoffs are

---

68 "Insider trading—What's the Problem?" CBC Online, December 21, 2005, http://www.cbc.ca/news/background/crime/insider_trading.html.
69 "Air Travel Trivia," *Skytrax*, Accessed September 12, 2010, http://www.airlinequality.com/main/facts.htm.

very demoralizing, not only for the poor employee who has been laid off (I have been, three times) but also for the workers who are left to pick up the slack.

There is a huge difference between laying people off because they are no longer needed and the now ubiquitous practice of laying people off to make the balance sheet balance, regardless of the consequences.

One of those consequences is that, in fact, you end up laying off customers. Or another way of looking at it, you end up laying off your customers. Here's another comment from Peter Joseph's movie Zeitgeist: Addendum:

> The path is clear, but our monetary based structure, which requires labor for income, blocks this progress, for humans need jobs in order to survive.[70]

---

[70] Peter Joseph, *Zeitgeist: Addendum*, (GMP, 2008), 2:03:07, http://vimeo.com/13770061.

Chapter 9
Volume and Saturation

Besides "greed," there are two words that I think define the scourge that led to a significant portion of our current Great Depression: volume and saturation. Let's first look at *volume*. Here's Webster's definition:

volume: (1) amount, (2) a considerable quantity[71]

There is likely not one CEO who would say that it is his or her responsibility to keep people employed. But when you don't understand volume, then when the volume of CEOs who take the layoff route to meet earnings forecasts reaches a critical mass, the end result is that too many people in the country are laid off. I would like to call this "The Cuber Syndrome."

The Cuber Syndrome occurs when the volume of laid-off, unemployed, and potentially soon-to-be-laid-off people reaches a critical mass that allows their behavior as a group to negatively affect such institutions as the economy. The laid-off people stop their discretionary spending for fear of going broke and/or not being able to meet the rent/mortgage payments. Coincident with that is that the layoffs cause some still-employed people to also stop their discretionary spending, in fear that they too may get laid off. In this instance, the group of people who stop spending as defined will be known as a Cuber Group.

We all need to save up something for that rainy day! It seems the

---

71   *Merriam-Webster Online*, s.v. "volume."

perfect storm is on the radar. As Peter Schiff wrote on the Euro Pacific Capital Inc. site in March 2009:

> Without a doubt, Americans, and all other people for that matter, benefit from having access to "rainy day money." But Americans should be saving for a rainy day, not adopting the attitude that if it rains I'll whip out my credit card. If Americans need to pay for a suddenly ill dog, to straighten their kid's teeth, or to pull them through a period of unemployment, they should save some of their present earnings. But saving money requires a reduction in spending, and that is something that modern economists, within and without the Administration, cannot abide.
>
> A drop in spending will create a sharper contraction in our economy—which is now comprised of 70% consumer spending. But this is no reason to discourage the process. The option to go into debt in the event of an emergency is no substitute for building personal savings for such events. Not only does such a strategy jeopardize the solvency of individuals or families when they are at their most vulnerable, but it deprives society of badly needed savings.[72]

In my humble, uneducated opinion, this nod toward saving—or its counterpart, the limiting of discretionary spending—will only end when people are comfortable that they may get a job or be able to retain their job. The odds of that don't look so good right now, according to these statistics from DailyFinance:

> Between December 2007 (when the recession officially began) and last month [July 2010], more than 8 million Americans have lost their jobs, according to

---

72 Peter Schiff, "Credit Card Cancer," Euro Pacific Capital Inc., March 13, 2009, http://www.europac.net/commentaries/credit_card_cancer.

the government. Of those job losses, 700,000 stem from layoffs at just 25 companies ...[73]

Let's take a look at those twenty-five companies, their ranking, their name, and the number of jobs cut since the recession began, from that same August 2009 DailyFinance article:

1. General Motors, 107,357
2. Citigroup, 73,056
3. Hewlett-Packard, 47,540
4. Circuit City Stores, 41,495
5. Merrill Lynch, 40,650
6. Verizon Wireless, 39,000
7. Pfizer, 31,771
8. Merck & Co., 24,400
9. Lehman Brothers, 23,340
10. Caterpillar, 23,024
11. JPMorgan Chase, 22,852
12. Starbucks, 21,316
13. AT&T, 18,401
14. Alcoa, 17,655
15. Dow Chemical, 17,530
16. DuPont, 17,000
17. Berkshire Hathaway, 16,900
18. Ford Motor, 15,912
19. KB Toys, 15,100
20. United States Postal Service, 15,000
21. DHL Express USA, 14,900
22. Sprint Nextel, 14,500
23. Sun Microsystems, 14,000
24. Boeing, 13,715
25. Chrysler, 13,672

For conspiracy-minded thinkers like me, I have to ask myself—how

---

[73] Douglas McIntyre, "The Layoff Kings: The 25 Companies Responsible for 700,000 Lost Jobs," *DailyFinance*, August 18, 2010, http://www.dailyfinance.com/story/the-layoff-kings-the-25-companies-responsible-for-700-000-lost/19588515/.

many of these layoffs were connected to the ability of the company to meet its profit targets and pay a dividend to the shareholders, thereby satisfying both the shareholders and Wall Street? This is cost cutting taken to an extreme. We can't keep doing this. And the punch line is that this is all driven by the investors—who may in fact be *you and me*, anyone who has purchased stock for the hope of making some money, especially when we have been promised that the money will be waiting for us under the Christmas tree when we retire.

My clout as an investor is nothing, especially compared to the high rollers mentioned throughout this book. The large investment firms hold the upper hand, in that if they do not like the profits that a company is making, they can pull their money out and invest it elsewhere. CEOs are hired to make sure that doesn't happen. And this creates the Catch-22[74] that is haunting us now—CEOs can't make the profit targets through their regular day-to-day business practices, so they resort to extreme cost-cutting measures and reach the low point of having to lay off their employees, and this unemployment reaches a critical mass (part of the Cuber Group) in which the unemployed stop spending, and now the companies can't make their profit targets through their regular day-to-day business, and the whole cycle starts again.

At the beginning of Chapter 8, Scott Richter, a portfolio manager at Fifth Third Asset Management, was quoted as saying, "Cost-cutting can help earnings in the short term, but it's not transformational."

According to Yale economist Robert Shiller, "Cost-cutting, some of it unsustainable, has boosted earnings lately." Shiller says you shouldn't avoid stocks, but "you shouldn't invest too much" in them, either.[75]

---

74   Joseph Heller, *Catch-22* (Simon & Schuster, 1961): "There was only one catch and that was Catch-22, which specified that a concern for one's safety in the face of dangers that were real and immediate was the process of a rational mind. Orr was crazy and could be grounded. All he had to do was ask; and as soon as he did, he would no longer be crazy and would have to fly more missions. Orr would be crazy to fly more missions and sane if he didn't, but if he was sane he had to fly them. If he flew them he was crazy and didn't have to; but if he didn't want to he was sane and had to. Yossarian was moved very deeply by the absolute simplicity of this clause of Catch-22 and let out a respectful whistle."

75   Steven Goldberg, "Robert Shiller Suggests a New Deal-Style Solution to Unemployment," *Kiplinger*, September 21, 2010, http://www.kiplinger.com/columns/value/archive/robert-shiller-suggests-a-new-deal-style-solution-unemployment.html.

There is a corollary to the Cuber Syndrome, which falls under the commonly used term "the domino effect." BusinessDictionary.com offers this definition:

> **domino effect**: Repercussion of an act or event under which every associated or connected entity is affected to more or less the same degree. Named after the circular arrangement of dominos in which if any one domino falls, all fall.[76]

Let me explain. In this day and age of the automakers getting their hands slapped for taking their private jets to Washington to ask for bailout money, we now have the problem that my industry, corporate communications, is seeing.

The corporate-communications industry is centered around live meetings or events—face to face, but on a much larger scale than in a boardroom. When the senior management of a company wants to speak to their sales force, employees, or perhaps a group of customers, these meetings can rival a rock concert in size and technical complexity. For some companies, this means that the main meeting might be held in a hockey arena to accommodate an audience of as much as 12,000 or more.

One of the reasons my industry is slowing down is because corporations do not want to be seen spending what could be perceived as "opulently." Webster gives this definition for "opulence":

> **opulence**: (1) wealth, affluence, (2) abundance, profusion[77]

I quit Wyeth in November of 2004 and moved from Philadelphia back to Toronto. From February of 2009 to the present, my streak of freelance work has all but evaporated. I had lunch with a friend who had a monthlong yearly gig in Las Vegas. In my industry, this is a lucrative gig. His gig was cancelled because the CEO thought it would be the "wrong optics." My associates in Europe keep commenting

---

76 *BusinessDictionary.com*, s.v. "domino effect," accessed February 12, 2010, http://www.businessdictionary.com/definition/domino-effect.html.
77 *Merriam-Webster Online*, s.v. "opulence."

on the number of shows that they are seeing canceled. Several North American production companies have had to resort to layoffs due to this slowdown in our sector.

If these corporate meetings are canceled, then there is a further domino effect that happens to the travel industry. This will mean fewer flights, fewer hotel bookings, and less catering—all substantial beneficiaries when business is booming. Based upon what happened to the airline industry after the events of September 2001, we know that the travel industry is fragile, and only time will tell at what point this and perhaps other industries will succumb to the current recession. So how does this get solved?

I had a horrific experience checking in for a flight recently, having to use the cattle-car line-up, and in this day and age of too few employees to service the quantity of customers, I was outraged. Then it occurred to me—the reason airline management is unaware of this service issue (because if they knew they would surely fix it) is because they don't have to check-in through the cattle-car line. They get to use the First Class line. And I remember thinking, "I wonder if these problems would exist if airline management had to use this line as well?"

I believe there is a direct correlation between this airline example and our ability to solve the financial crisis. Those who have been tasked with solving the financial crisis aren't in a position where they are worried about their personal cash running out. They have no fear about making next month's mortgage payment or the minimum payment on their Visa bill—or I guess in their case the Amex bill—or health costs. So they cannot empathize with the likes of you and me, who are desperately afraid.

Their fearlessness would be, perhaps, admirable if we were in the army, where generals lead their troops into dire situations and, like Patton, convince everyone that everything will be *okay* and really, it's good for you. The troops see their leader facing the same possible outcome: death. Imagine your "boss" on the front line, possibly taking the ultimate hit, not hiding over a map miles away from the action. But we are not in the army. The people I know have their bank accounts near empty, their debt is suffocating them, and they live in fear of no employment. When I look for a guiding light, a visionary, someone to lead us out of this financial crisis, who truly understands this predicament, all I see are a bunch of greedy "experts" on Wall Street who only care about when they can get back to making more millions, not about addressing the real problems. This behavior is what I would like to term "The Gauthier Principle."

The Gauthier Principle will be defined as: An affluent person or group of persons tasked with trying to fix a problem of which one part or symptom of that problem is a threat to their own affluence. They become sidetracked from the real problem by their desire to fix the symptom that is a threat to their affluence. Regardless of them recognizing or not recognizing the real problem, they will not divert from their strategy of solving the threat to their affluence. Generally, they will make you feel that their symptom is the real problem. Ultimately, their symptom cannot be fixed without addressing the real problem.

Does this sound like anyone you know?

As mentioned earlier, another key that I feel led to Great Depression II is *saturation*. Webster gives this definition:

> **saturation:** (1) a state of maximum impregnation: as a complete infiltration, (2) the supplying of a market with as much of a product as it will absorb, (3) an overwhelming concentration of military forces or firepower[78]

Can't we add more items to their list, such as:

> (4) an overwhelming concentration of flat-screen TVs, (5) an overwhelming concentration of gas-guzzling cars that no one wants, (6) an overwhelming concentration of products made in China that will inevitably end up in the landfill

Okay, I feel better now. I think I've gotten my point across.

Companies have marketing departments that determine what the consumer potential is for the purchase of their products, and then those companies, as discussed, make forecasts, not only for the "experts" on Wall Street but for their own production and other internal issues. Consumerism is a gold mine! And while we were all drunk on

---

[78] *Merriam-Webster Online*, s.v. "saturation."

consumerism, it seemed like the bar would never close. Do you still have a twenty-four-hour Home Depot in your city?

So now that we are sobering up (*please, just one more drink*), we get to ask—how can all this forecasting go so wrong? What happens when a company finds itself with too much stock in inventory, stored in the warehouse? An Associated Press article from March 2009 provides one example:

> Bankruptcy experts are urging a congressional subcommittee to reexamine the bankruptcy law changes they say helped Circuit City and other companies go under and cut hundreds of thousands of jobs.
>
> The House Commercial and Administrative Law Subcommittee heard testimony today on why federal bankruptcy protection didn't save the Henrico County-based consumer electronics retailer, which laid off about 34,000 workers.
>
> Circuit City closed its 567 remaining U.S. stores Sunday. It filed for protection in November to address heightened competition, pressure from vendors and waning consumer spending.
>
> Witnesses said that on top of general economic conditions, provisions enacted in 2005 to speed reorganization forced Circuit City out of business. [79]

Let's highlight the five reasons they've listed for Circuit City's demise:

1. Heightened competition;
2. Pressure from vendors;
3. Waning consumer spending;

---

[79] Michael Felberbaum, "Congressional Panel Examines Circuit City Bankruptcy," *Richmond Times-Dispatch*, March 11, 2009, http://www.timesdispatch.com/rtd/news/local/article/CIRCGAT11_20090311-163002/229000/.

4. General economic conditions; and last, but not least,
5. Provisions enacted in 2005 to speed reorganization.

I love the phrase "waning consumer spending." That point seems to be the highlight to me, but what do I know.

There is no bar graph or pie chart to let us know just how much each of these five excuses played a part in the collapse of Circuit City.

Through the fall and Christmas period of 2008, I was avidly shopping for a flat-screen TV. I checked the flyers; I went online; I did my research. It really seemed that no retailer was going to budge from its pricing, and all the pricing was similar between the big guns—Best Buy, Circuit City, and in Canada, Future Shop. It was a staring contest between the retailers and the consumers. I held out until I went into the outlet store of a smaller retailer named 2001 Audio Video and got a great deal on a top-of-the-line Sharp Aquos, "last year's model." This gave me a benchmark as I continued to follow the pricing, to see at what point the retailers would say, "Enough already, *okay*, we're ready to really discount these things to get them moving." I never saw that happen. Not even during the after-Christmas sales. In Canada, that is usually the best time to get a deal.

I guess I could say "kudos" to the retailers for holding out for their margin. But it will be difficult to get sympathy from me when they go bankrupt. The prices on those same models dropped substantially when the new-and-improved "240 hertz" and "LED" flat screens suddenly hit the market. My flat screen can be bought for half of what I paid for it two years ago, but alas, that's the way technology bounces!

Chapter 10
Outsourcing

Another seemingly effective cost-cutting measure is the ever-so-popular sport called *outsourcing*. The early stages of outsourcing involved dismantling a department of full-timers and giving the work to a contractor who paid its employees substantially less and took on the healthcare, insurance, and other HR headaches.

The biggest accounting trick here is that even if it did cost the same amount, or in some cases more, the outsourced expenses showed up in a different line item on the balance sheet and therefore made the bottom line look much better than it really was.

In the old days, one of the first departments to be outsourced was the multimedia department (or the video department before the days of multimedia). "Multi Media" was the department I worked in at Wyeth. Wyeth was a bit of an anomaly because not only did it still have a multimedia department, but one that was staffed with very talented people. One key element we used to justify our existence was a cost-reporting method that would use real-world numbers to show how much a project would have cost if it had been outsourced. We tried to be as fair and accurate as possible in generating these numbers. For instance, the video department, headed up by my friend MB, would produce world-class videos for $5,000. These videos would cost somewhere from $60,000 to $100,000 in the open market. If you're producing twelve of these videos a year, the savings can justify the investment. There was also a photography department headed up by my now-retired buddy Walt, a print and interactive department, and my domain—the computer-graphics department and special-events department.

I mentioned earlier that sometimes it does cost more to outsource. Multimedia is definitely an area that will cost more to outsource, but again, those costs now show up as a different line item on the balance sheet and therefore make the bottom line look better despite the increase in cost.

Cost-cutting can only go so far … or can it? Many CEOs will just keep cutting, regardless of the consequences, so that Wall Street will be happy with their performance and treat them nice.

If the bottom line is carved as close to the bone as possible, what are the next steps for a CEO looking to meet the forecasts? Now is the time to introduce outsourcing to foreign countries. This outsourcing exercise has "cheap labor" as the mantra, although there are risks involved. Many companies have done this—some successfully, some not so much, and some still undecided.

It seems that anyone in Canada who uses Bell Canada as an Internet service provider is aware that Bell's call centre is based in India. India has the reputation as the first place that these call centers and departments are being outsourced to. But what happens when the CEO needs to take even further drastic action to try to meet the forecasts? A 2005 article from the *Inquirer* offers one scenario:

> Number crunchers at Gartner are predicting doom and gloom for the Indian outsourcing biz.
>
> The Big G says that India's wage bill for developers is sky rocketing and its share of the outsourcing market could fall by as much as 45 percent by 2007.
>
> Gartner says that the ancient land is having to face stiff competition from cheaper, or closer countries such

as the Philippines, Malaysia, Vietnam and Eastern Europe and they will not cut the mustard.

The main reason is that India's wage bill is getting too high, with call centre staff now demanding between $159-$204 a month when before they only wanted $114-$136.

At the same time the country's infrastructure is not keeping pace with the rapid growth of the industry.[80]

India's wages are now considered *too expensive* at $200 per month per employee. Norman Lear, the award-winning TV producer of such shows as *All in the Family*, comments in a March 2009 *Huffington Post* entry on the insanity of satisfying shareholders:

> ... the systemic disease that got us here: short-term thinking; the lunatic need for a profit statement this quarter considerably larger than the last, at the expense of every other value.[81]

Capitalism works well when the going is good and works good if you are on the side of the good going. But the Constitution of the United States of America does not include the constitution of other countries. Would it still be capitalism and free enterprise if we were to put limits on the way foreign businesses can do business in America? Anyone who does business in America is the beneficiary of this national American economy, and therefore has—or should have—a responsibility to this great American economy, the American people, and the communities.

If foreign companies are allowed to do business within the borders

---

80 Nick Farrell, "Indian Outsourcing Too Expensive," *Inquirer*, August 25, 2005, http://www.theinquirer.net/inquirer/news/1040943/indian-outsourcing-too-expensive. Copyrighted 2010. Incisive Media. 72353-12M:N10SH.
81 Norman Lear, "Come, Shoot the Messengers!" *Huffington Post*, March 19, 2009, http://www.huffingtonpost.com/norman-lear/come-shoot-the-messengers_b_176692.html.

of America without having some type of commitment to the economy, the people, and the communities, they can wreak whatever financial and cultural devastation they want, take our dollars out of the country, and leave us without jobs.

Perhaps America could take a lesson from—holy crap!—the Chinese, who do not allow foreign companies to go into their proposed businesses in China without a Chinese joint-venture partner at 49 percent.

Following is a transcript from a July 2009 episode of the CNN show *Lou Dobbs Tonight*, part of Lou's "Exporting America" series. It is an interview with Atul Vashistha, founder of neoIT, who had just hosted a conference the previous month for American companies. It was a seminar to teach American corporate executives how to ship jobs overseas. I include this transcript not just for the outsourcing implications, but for the attitude Vashistha shows toward foreign companies being able to take advantage of America not protecting America:

> **Lou Dobbs**: [Vashistha] says globalization will ultimately help us all. That offshore outsourcing is not to blame for the loss of jobs in this country. I am now joined by Atul Vashistha. He says it's a misconception. And how is it a misconception?
>
> **Atul Vashistha**: It's a misconception because if you look at what offshore outsourcing is doing for America, it is actually helping American companies stay competitive. It is helping them lower the cost of products and services, and actually it's improving the buying power in our nation.
>
> **Lou Dobbs**: I think I understand, if you will, the premise of what you're saying. But when we watch, and as we document here, literally, hundreds of thousands of jobs being shipped to cheap overseas labor markets, those jobs are replaced typically by salaries that are 30 percent lower. And there is no migration up the

value chain; it's down the value chain. So how does that help America?

Atul Vashistha: You know, Lou, there is no denying that in the short term we have a problem. And I think the industry, the government, and the companies are still not doing enough. What I can tell you is that our clients are starting to do things to combat that.

Lou Dobbs: Like what?

Atul Vashistha: For example, some of the things our clients are doing is they're actually putting money into retraining. We cannot be competitive in this new global economy if our workers don't continue to update their skills. Even if you are a software programmer ...

Lou Dobbs: Let me ask you this. Engineering [and] software programming have unemployment rates approaching double digits in this country. What in the world are you going to train them for?

Atul Vashistha: Lou, technology as you know is changing every year. ["*I do indeed.*"] If four years ago you were doing HTML or Web-based programming, you need to do a lot of different things today because that technology is old now. I did my engineering degree and my MBA. I went back to Harvard last year to educate myself again. And I think that's something we absolutely have to do.

Lou Dobbs: That's boffo. But let's talk about those hundreds of thousands of jobs. People glibly talk about training, men and women who have trained themselves in a variety of skills, who have a variety of educational pursuits and degrees. I hear people start talking about training as if that's sort of a panacea.

What jobs should they train themselves for? We are shipping high-value jobs overseas to India, to the Philippines, to Ireland, to Poland, to Russia for crying out loud. What in the world are we suppose to train them to do? Now, I understand the profit motive—as a matter of fact, no one's more pro-business, pro-American free enterprise than I am. But I am also pro-American worker. You talk about pain. We are seeing evidence of it every day.

Atul Vashistha: But Lou, if we don't focus on R&D investment in training, we can't just put up our borders and imagine that these jobs will stay. In fact, companies are going bankrupt because they're not taking advantage of these lower cost markets.

Lou Dobbs: Because somebody else is? Is that right?

Atul Vashistha: Right, exactly ...

Lou Dobbs: So what you end up [with] is a "race to the bottom" as it has been styled, because if one company is going over to India to get a job to pay a salary that is a tenth of what they would be paying in this country, they're forced to compete. This is not free trade. This is not comparative advantage as envisioned by David Ricardo [in his 1817 book, *On the Principles of Political Economy and Taxation*]. This is the wholesale exportation of American wealth.

Atul Vashistha: But Lou, the difference here is that this is a global economy. We can't imagine ...

Lou Dobbs: I understand that. But these are all "saws." Globalization has been a fact since 1987, for crying out loud.

Atul Vashistha: And Lou, take a look at what has happened to the buying power in our country. It's significantly gone up. And I know, in the last two years, three years …

Lou Dobbs: Earnings in this country and consumption power in this country for the last three decades have declined—over the past three years has actually fallen even more dramatically than that average over three decades. It's quite the inverse.

Atul Vashistha: Lou, I'm sorry, I beg to differ. ["*Please.*"] If you take a look at the buying power of our country, let's take a look at the last two decades. We created 22 million excess jobs than were destroyed in our country. This is the Bureau of Labor Statistics number for the last two decades.

Lou Dobbs: We created 22 million jobs during the course of the Clinton administration from 1992 to 2000.

Atul Vashistha: Right. So we created surplus jobs. So what I am talking about is, as the economy changed, we actually created more jobs than we lost. At the same time, the buying power …

Lou Dobbs: That's sort of evident, would we say, 22 million jobs.

Atul Vashistha: What is happening today is, I think this is the next evolution in the global economy.

Lou Dobbs: That's wonderful. Great evolution—if you believe that the United States should be shipping its wealth, its jobs, its standard of living, and its quality of life to Third World countries where there are no regulations for environment, no regulations for labor, no standards that is a requirement here in this country. The logical extrapolation tool is that if we are going to compete fairly, with fair trade on a globalized market, it seems to me that India, the Philippines, Mexico, Central American nations, should have the same standards—otherwise we are competing simply on the price of labor.

Atul Vashistha: Lou, I absolutely agree with you. In fact, if you look at the service industry which we participate in, these companies are paying higher average wages than the local counterparts. If you look at what is happening in India and China …

Lou Dobbs: Whoa, whoa, whoa … You're saying American companies are paying higher wages in other countries than native companies.

Atul Vashistha: American companies and the local companies that participate in this business, so companies like MphasiS, or Wipro, all these companies in India, they are paying better wages than the average people get in that country.

Lou Dobbs: The average Indian company. But why in the world do ten million Americans who are unemployed in this country give a damn.

Atul Vashistha: Well Lou, here is why they give a damn. Because if we don't do this, if we don't continue to innovate and let our companies be successful, we will lose more jobs in the future.

Lou Dobbs: Whoa, whoa, whoa, whoa … Wait a minute, wait a minute. You're not innovating. You're not being more efficient. You're talking about hiring cheaper labor. Those are only code words for cheap labor. McKinsey did a study, as you are aware of, in what is the bulk of the gain for American companies—it's all from labor savings.

Atul Vashistha: A bulk, but don't forget the other reason ...

Lou Dobbs: The bulk, as in 70 percent of it.

Atul Vashistha: Right, Lou, but what happens to the money that comes back to our country? ["*What money?*"] The money that's being repatriated back to the country. The savings that happened for American companies.

Lou Dobbs: We should ship all our jobs then, 'cause it sounds like a highly profitable enterprise.

Atul Vashistha: Lou, it's easy to take a look at that ...

Lou Dobbs: Atul, I understand your position, I understand the profit mode, but corporations have a stake in this country, do they not? ["*I absolutely agree.*"] And they have a stake in the community, in investing in their people; they have a responsibility because they're the beneficiary of this national American economy.

Atul Vashistha: Lou, I absolutely agree with you. In fact, one of the things that has not happened yet, is that the industry and the associations and the companies have not come together to address the displaced workers. Now I can tell you like I was telling you before, some of our companies are doing that apart from training …

Lou Dobbs: That's a wonderful paternal outlook, you know, but what I would much prefer to hear business people, men and woman in this country running corporations, and folks like you trying to make a dollar—you have a responsibility to this national economy. This is not just a marketplace—it's a nation. Right?[82]

For the lengths that America goes to protect its borders from illegal workers—illegal workers who might take American jobs away from Americans—it seems ironic that we let foreign companies set up shop right in our backyard, and give our jobs to those same foreigners that we are so militant about not letting into our country. When a foreigner takes your job, does it really matter whether they are standing on your soil or their soil? Either way, they got your job. There is no corporate equivalent of the U.S. Citizenship and Immigration Services (USCIS), U.S. Immigration and Customs Enforcement (ICE), and U.S. Customs and Border Protection (CBP). I'm suggesting that a fictitious government department, bearing the acronym PAFFCL (Protecting America From Foreign Corporate Looting), could protect America from foreign corporations who set up shop in America. PAFFCL's job would be to set up by-laws and boundaries with these foreign companies, so that after the initial romance with employing Americans to get established, these companies don't just turn around and outsource the jobs to foreign countries that utilize cheap labor with little or no human rights, while still benefiting from the American economy.

So if America needs to protect itself from foreign corporate looting, I need to be fair to the foreign looters, and implicate our own heroic American companies who have looted the economy by outsourcing American jobs to foreign countries.

In another episode of its "Exporting America" series (circa 2004), CNN's *Lou Dobbs Tonight* compiled a confirmed list of 791 US

---

82 Atul Vashistha, interview by Lou Dobbs, *Lou Dobbs Tonight*, CNN, July 27, 2009, accessed November 13, 2010, http://www.youtube.com/watch?v=N1ohZET0qR8.

companies that were either sending American jobs overseas or choosing to employ cheap overseas labor instead of American workers. Here is that list:

3Com
3M
Aalfs Manufacturing
Aavid Thermal Technologies
ABC-NACO
Accenture
Access Electronics
Accuride Corporation
Accuride International
Adaptec
ADC
Adobe Systems
Advanced Energy Industries
Aetna
Affiliated Computer Services
AFS Technologies
A.G. Edwards
Agere Systems
Agilent Technologies
AIG
Alamo Rent A Car
Albany International Corp.
Albertson's
Alcoa
Alcoa Fujikura
Allen Systems Group
Alliance Semiconductor
Allstate
Alpha Thought Global
Altria Group
Amazon.com
AMD
Americ Disc
American Dawn

American Express
American Greetings
American Household
American Management Systems
American Standard
American Uniform Company
AMETEK
AMI DODUCO
Amloid Corporation
Amphenol Corporation
Analog Devices
Anchor Glass Container
ANDA Networks
Anderson Electrical Products
Andrew Corporation
Anheuser-Busch
Angelica Corporation
Ansell Health Care
Ansell Protective Products
Anvil Knitwear
AOL
A.O. Smith
Apple
Applied Materials
Ark-Les Corporation
Arlee Home Fashions
Art Leather Manufacturing
Artex International
ArvinMeritor
Asco Power Technologies
Ashland
AstenJohnson
Asyst Technologies
Atchison Products, Inc.
A.T. Cross Company
AT&T
AT&T Wireless
A.T. Kearney
Augusta Sportswear

Authentic Fitness Corporation
Automatic Data Processing
Avanade
Avanex
Avaya
Avery Dennison
Azima Healthcare Services
Axiohm Transaction Solutions
Bank of America
Bank of New York
Bank One
Bard Access Systems
Barnes Group
Barth & Dreyfuss of California
Bassett Furniture
Bassler Electric Company
BBi Enterprises L.P.
Beacon Blankets
BearingPoint
Bear Stearns
BEA Systems
Bechtel
Becton Dickinson
BellSouth
Bentley Systems
Berdon LLP
Berne Apparel
Bernhardt Furniture
Best Buy
Bestt Liebco Corporation
Beverly Enterprises
Birdair, Inc.
BISSELL
Black & Decker
Blauer Manufacturing
Blue Cast Denim
Bobs Candies
Borden Chemical
Bourns

Bose Corporation
Bowater
BMC Software
Boeing
Braden Manufacturing
Briggs Industries
Brady Corporation
Bristol-Myers Squibb
Bristol Tank & Welding Co.
Brocade
Brooks Automation
Brown Wooten Mills Inc.
Buck Forkardt, Inc.
Bumble Bee
Burle Industries
Burlington House Home Fashions
Burlington Northern and Santa Fe Railway
Cadence Design Systems
Camfil Farr
Candle Corporation
Cains Pickles
Capital One
Cardinal Brands
Carrier
Carter's
Caterpillar
C-COR.net
C&D Technologies
Cellpoint Systems
Cendant
Centis, Inc.
Cerner Corporation
Charles Schwab
ChevronTexaco
The Cherry Corporation
CIBER
Ciena
Cigna
Circuit City

Cirrus Logic
Cisco Systems
Citigroup
Clear Pine Mouldings
Clorox
CNA
Coastcast Corp.
Coca-Cola
Cognizant Technology Solutions
Collins & Aikman
Collis, Inc.
Columbia House
Comcast Holdings
Comdial Corporation
Computer Associates
Computer Horizons
Computer Sciences Corporation
CompuServe
Concise Fabricators
Conectl Corporation
Conseco
Consolidated Metro
Continental Airlines
Convergys
Cooper Crouse-Hinds
Cooper Tire & Rubber
Cooper Tools
Cooper Wiring Devices
Copperweld
Cordis Corporation
Corning
Corning Cable Systems
Corning Frequency Control
Countrywide Financial
COVAD Communications
Covansys
Creo Americas
Cross Creek Apparel
Crouzet Corporation

Crown Holdings
CSX
Cummins
Cutler-Hammer
Cypress Semiconductor
Dana Corporation
Daniel Woodhead
Davis Wire Corp.
Daws Manufacturing
Dayton Superior
DeCrane Aircraft
Delco Remy
Dell Computer
DeLong Sportswear
Delphi
Delta Air Lines
Delta Apparel
Direct TV
Discover
DJ Orthopedics
Document Sciences Corporation
Dometic Corp.
Donaldson Company
Douglas Furniture of California
Dow Chemical
Dresser
Dun & Bradstreet
DuPont
Earthlink
Eastman Kodak
Eaton Corporation
Edco, Inc.
Editorial America
eFunds
Edscha
Ehlert Tool Company
Elbeco Inc.
Electroglas
Electronic Data Systems

Electronics for Imaging
Electro Technology
Eli Lilly
Elmer's Products
E-Loan
EMC
Emerson Electric
Emerson Power Transmission
Emglo Products
Engel Machinery
En Pointe Technologies
Equifax
Ernst & Young
Essilor of America
Ethan Allen
Evenflo
Evergreen Wholesale Florist
Evolving Systems
Evy of California
Expedia
Extrasport
ExxonMobil
Fairfield Manufacturing
Fair Isaac
Fansteel Inc.
Farley's & Sathers Candy Co.
Fasco Industries
Fawn Industries
Fayette Cotton Mill
FCI USA
Fedders Corporation
Federal Mogul
Federated Department Stores
Fellowes
Fender Musical Instruments
Fidelity Investments
Financial Techologies International
Findlay Industries
First American Title Insurance

First Data
First Index
Fisher Hamilton
Flowserve
Fluor
FMC Corporation
Fontaine International
Ford Motor
Foster Wheeler
Franklin Mint
Franklin Templeton
Freeborders
Frito Lay
Fruit of the Loom
Garan Manufacturing
Gateway
GE Capital
GE Medical Systems
Gemtron Corporation
General Binding Corporation
General Cable Corp.
General Electric
General Motors
Generation 2 Worldwide
Genesco
Georgia-Pacific
Gerber Childrenswear
GlobespanVirata
Goldman Sachs
Gold Toe Brands
Goodrich
Goodyear Tire & Rubber
Google
Graphic Controls
Greenpoint Mortgage
Greenwood Mills
Grote Industries
Grove U.S. LLC
Guardian Life Insurance

Guilford Mills
Gulfstream Aerospace Corp.
Haggar
Halliburton
Hamilton Beach/Procter-Silex
The Hartford Financial Services Group
Harper-Wyman Company
Hasbro Manufacturing Services
Hawk Corporation
Hawker Power Systems, Inc.
Haworth
Headstrong
HealthAxis
Hedstrom
Hein-Werner Corp.
Helen of Troy
Helsapenn Inc.
Hershey
Hewitt Associates
Hewlett-Packard
Hoffman Enclosures, Inc.
Hoffman/New Yorker
The Holmes Group
Home Depot
Honeywell
HSN
Hubbell Inc.
Humana
Hunter Sadler
Hutchinson Sealing Systems, Inc
HyperTech Solutions
IBM
iGate Corporation
Illinois Tool Works
IMI Cornelius
Imperial Home Decor Group
Indiana Knitwear Corp.
IndyMac Bancorp
Infogain

Ingersoll-Rand
Innodata Isogen
Innova Solutions
Insilco Technologies
Intel
InterMetro Industries
International Paper
Interroll Corporation
Intuit
Invacare
Iris Graphics, Inc.
Isola Laminate Systems
Iteris Holdings, Inc.
ITT Educational Services
ITT Industries
Jabil Circuit
Jacobs Engineering
Jacuzzi
Jakel, Inc.
JanSport
Jantzen Inc.
JDS Uniphase
Jockey International
John Crane
John Deere
Johns Manville
Johnson Controls
Johnson & Johnson
JPMorgan Chase
J.R. Simplot
Juniper Networks
Justin Brands
KANA Software
Kaiser Permanente
Kanbay
Kayby Mills of North Carolina
Keane
Kellogg
Kellwood

KEMET
KEMET Electronics
Kendall Healthcare
Kenexa
Kentucky Apparel
Kerr-McGee Chemical
KeyCorp
Key Industries
Key Safety Systems
Key Tronic Corp.
Kimberly-Clark
KLA-Tencor
Knight Textile Corp.
Kojo Worldwide Corporation
Kraft Foods
K2 Inc.
Kulicke and Soffa Industries
Kwikset
Lancer Partnership
Lander Company
LaCrosse Footwear
Lamb Technicon
Lau Industries
Lands' End
Lawson Software
Layne Christensen
Leach International
Lear Corporation
Leech Tool & Die Works
Lehman Brothers
Leoni Wiring Systems
Levi Strauss
Leviton Manufacturing Co.
Lexmark International
Lexstar Technologies
Liebert Corporation
Lifescan
Lillian Vernon
Linksys

Linq Industrial Fabrics, Inc.
Lionbridge Technologies
Lionel
Littelfuse
LiveBridge
LNP Engineering Plastics
Lockheed Martin
Longaberger
Louisiana-Pacific Corporation
Louisville Ladder Group LLC
Lowe's
Lucent
Lund International
Lyall Alabama
Madill Corporation
Magma Design Automation
Magnequench
Magnetek
Maidenform
Mallinckrodt, Inc.
The Manitowoc Company
Manugistics
Marathon Oil
Maritz
Mars
Marshall Fields
Mattel
Master Lock
Materials Processing, Inc.
Maxim Integrated Products
Maxi Switch
Maxxim Medical
Maytag
McDATA Corporation
McKinsey & Company
MeadWestvaco
Mediacopy
Medtronic
Mellon Bank

Mentor Graphics Corp.
Meridian Automotive Systems
Merit Abrasive Products
Merrill Corporation
Merrill Lynch
Metasolv
MetLife
Micro Motion, Inc.
Microsoft
Midcom Inc.
Midwest Electric Products
Milacron
Modern Plastics Technics
Modine Manufacturing
Moen
Money's Foods Us Inc.
Monona Wire Corp.
Monsanto
Morgan Stanley
Motion Control Industries
Motor Coach Industries International
Motorola
Mrs. Allison's Cookie Co.
Mulox
Nabco
Nabisco
NACCO Industries
National City Corporation
National Electric Carbon Products
National Life
National Semiconductor
NCR Corporation
neoIT
NETGEAR
Network Associates
Newell Rubbermaid
Newell Window Furnishings
New World Pasta
New York Life Insurance

Nice Ball Bearings
Nike
Nordstrom
Northrop Grumman
Northwest Airlines
Nu Gro Technologies
Nu-kote International
NutraMax Products
Nypro Alabama
O'Bryan Brothers Inc.
Ocwen Financial
Office Depot
Ogden Manufacturing
Oglevee, Ltd
Ohio Art
Ohmite Manufacturing Co.
Old Forge Lamp & Shade
Omniglow Corporation
ON Semiconductor
Orbitz
Oracle
OshKosh B'Gosh
Otis Elevator
Outsource Partners International
Owens-Brigam Medical Co.
Owens Corning
Oxford Automotive
Oxford Industries
Pacific Precision Metals
Pak-Mor Manufacturing
palmOne
Parallax Power Components
Paramount Apparel
Parker-Hannifin
Parsons E&C
Paxar Corporation
Pearson Digital Learning
Peavey Electronics CorporationÊÊ
PeopleSoft

PepsiCo
Pericom Semiconductor
PerkinElmer
PerkinElmer Life Sciences, Inc.
Perot Systems
Pfaltzgraff
Pfizer
Phillips-Van Heusen
Pinnacle West Capital Corporation
Pitney Bowes
Plaid Clothing Company
Planar Systems
Plexus
Pliant Corporation
PL Industries
Polaroid
Polymer Sealing Solutions
Portal Software
Portex, Inc.
Portola Packaging
Port Townsend Paper Corp.
Power One
Pratt & Whitney
Price Pfister
priceline.com
Pridecraft Enterprises
Prime Tanning
Primus Telecom
Procter & Gamble
Progress Lighting
ProQuest
Providian Financial
Prudential Insurance
Quaker Oats
Quadion Corporation
Quantegy
Quark
Qwest Communications
Radio Flyer

Radio Shack
Rainbow Technologies
Rawlings Sporting Goods
Rayovac
Raytheon Aircraft
RCG Information Technology
Red Kap
Regal-Beloit Corporation
Regal Rugs
Respiratory Support Products
Regence Group
R.G. Barry Corp.
Rich Products
River Holding Corp.
Robert Mitchell Co., Inc.
Rockwell Automations
Rockwell Collins
Rogers
Rohm & Haas
Ropak Northwest
RR Donnelley & Sons
Rugged Sportswear
Russell Corporation
S1 Corporation
S & B Engineers and Constructors
Sabre
Safeway
SAIC
Sallie Mae
Samsonite
Samuel-Whittar, Inc.
Sanford
Sanmina-SCI
Sapient
Sara Lee
Saturn Electronics & Engineering
SBC Communications
Schumacher Electric
Scientific Atlanta

Seal Glove Manufacturing
Seco Manufacturing Co.
SEI Investments
Sequa Corporation
Seton Company
Sheldahl Inc.
Shipping Systems, Inc.
Siebel Systems
Sierra Atlantic
Sights Denim Systems, Inc.
Signal Transformer
Signet Armorlite, Inc
Sikorsky
Silicon Graphics
Simula Automotive SafetyÊ
SITEL
Skyworks Solutions
SMC Networks
SML Labels
SNC Manufacturing CompanyÊ
SoftBrands
Sola Optical USA
Solectron
Sonoco Products Co.
Southwire Company
Sovereign Bancorp
Spectrum Control
Spicer Driveshaft Manufacturing
Springs Industries
Springs Window Fashions
Sprint
Sprint PCS
SPX Corporation
Square D
Standard Textile Co.
Stanley Furniture
Stanley Works
Stant Manufacturing
Starkist Seafood

State Farm Insurance
State Street
Steelcase
StorageTek
StrategicPoint Investment Advisors
Strattec Security Corp.
STS Apparel Corporation
Summitville Tiles
Sun Microsystems
Sunrise Medical
SunTrust Banks
Superior Uniform Group
Supra Telecom
Sure Fit
SurePrep
The Sutherland Group
Sweetheart Cup Co.
Swift Denim
Sykes Enterprises
Symbol Technologies
Synopsys
Synygy
Takata Retraint Systems
Target
Teccor Electronics
Techalloy Company, Inc.
Technotrim
Tecumseh
Tee Jays Manufacturing
Telcordia
Telect
Teleflex
TeleTech
Telex Communications
Tellabs
Tenneco Automotive
Teradyne
Texaco Exploration and Production
Texas Instruments

Textron
Thermal Industries
Therm-O-Disc, Inc.
Thomas & Betts
Thomasville Furniture
Thomas Saginaw Ball Screw Co.
Three G's Manufacturing Co.
Thrivent Financial for Lutherans
Time Warner
Tingley Rubber Corp.
The Timken Company
The Toro Company
Tomlinson Industries
Tower Automotive
Toys "R" Us
Trailmobile Trailer
Trans-Apparel Group
TransPro, Inc.
Trans Union
Travelocity
Trek Bicycle Corporation
Trend Technologies
TriMas Corp.
Trinity Industries
Triquint Semiconductor
TriVision Partners
Tropical Sportswear
TRW Automotive
Tumbleweed Communications
Tupperware
Tyco Electronics
Tyco International
UCAR Carbon Company
Underwriters Laboratories
UniFirst Corporation
Union Pacific Railroad
Unison Industries
Unisys
United Airlines

UnitedHealth Group Inc.
United Online
United Plastics Group
United States Ceramic Tile
United Technologies
Universal Lighting Technologies
USAA
Valence Technology
Valeo Climate Control
VA Software
Velvac
Vertiflex Products
Veritas
Verizon
VF Corporation
Viasystems
Vishay
Visteon
VITAL Sourcing
Wabash Alloys, L.L.C.
Wabash Technologies
Wachovia Bank
Walgreens
Walls Industries
Warnaco
Washington Group International
Washington Mutual
WebEx
WellChoice
Wellman Thermal Systems
Walls Industries
Werner Co.
West Corporation
Weavexx
Weiser Lock
West Point Stevens

Weyerhaeuser
Whirlpool
White Rodgers
Williamson-Dickie Manufacturing Company
Winpak Films
Wolverine World Wide
Woodstock Wire Works
WorldCom
World Kitchen
Wyeth
Wyman-Gordon Forgings
Xerox
Xpectra Incorporated
Xpitax
Yahoo!
Yarway Corporation
York International
Zenith
ZettaWorks[83]

Now *that* is one overwhelming list.

Included in that list is my former employer, Wyeth Pharmaceuticals (now Pfizer). I can vouch for Wyeth—not in the manufacturing sense (although they too have plants around the world), but in the fact that they outsourced their accounts payable department to India. It was an apparent fiasco. The president responsible ended up resigning over it. I had one of my freelance invoices go temporarily missing in the melee.

Since the merger with Pfizer, my friends in the interactive department wait every day for news about their apparent outsourcing, although at least it will be to a local American firm.

Capitalism starts to show its flaws when we get into the recession we are in now. There is little or no talk about changing the laws of capitalism or protecting America from the foreign countries that compete on an unlevel playing field, so our CEOs will need to keep

---

[83] "Lou Dobbs Tonight—Exporting America," CNN, Accessed March 7, 2011, http://www.cnn.com/CNN/Programs/lou.dobbs.tonight/popups/exporting.america/ content.html.

resorting to their harsh and sometimes irrational practices to keep making their profit targets.

What drives the greed that makes a CEO take such harsh actions as outsourcing to meet a bottom line? According to Peter Joseph's *Zeitgeist: Addendum*:

> These people don't have to get together and plot to do things. They all basically work under one primary assumption, and that is that they must maximize profits regardless of the social and environmental costs.[84]

And here, in a July 2009 ABC News report, Paul Krugman draws the direct correlation between the recession, the unemployed, and the stimulus plan:

> Nobel-Prize winning economist Paul Krugman said the nation is on course for a "prolonged jobless" economic recovery unless the Obama administration steps in with a second round of government stimulus money. "The fact of the matter is that the unemployment rate is much worse than the administration contemplated or that most people expected," Krugman told ABC News. "So the economy is much weaker than we thought it'd be, meaning, in fact, it could use more stimulus."[85]

Now it's time to put on a thicker skin for the next chapter—a discussion about stock options.

---

84 Peter Joseph, *Zeitgeist: Addendum* (GMP, 2008), 2:03:07, http://vimeo.com/13770061.
85 Jennifer Parker, "Krugman: U.S. Headed for 'Jobless' Recovery," ABC News, July 1, 2009, http://abcnews.go.com/ThisWeek/Politics/story?id=7966402&page=1.

Chapter 11
Stock Options, or Legal Counterfeiting

Of all the social institutions we are born into, directed by and conditioned upon, there seems to be no system as taken for granted, and misunderstood, as the monetary system. Taking on nearly religious proportions, the established monetary institution exists as one of the most unquestioned forms of faith there is. How money is created, the policies by which it is governed, and how it truly affects society, are unregistered interests of the great majority of the population.[86]

—*Peter Joseph, Zeitgeist: Addendum*

One of the most misunderstood elements of financial instability is the *stock option*. Now it is likely that you will find people who disagree with me here, but they are likely to be the ones who stand to make the most from those stock options. Stock options, in my mind, are the equivalent of legal counterfeiting. People see huge windfalls from their stock options without having had to do much to earn them.

---

86 Peter Joseph, *Zeitgeist: Addendum* (GMP, 2008), 2:03:07, http://vimeo.com/13770061.

What is a stock option (just in case you don't know)? Let me try to help you understand:

Let's say I own a company that is listed on the stock market with a share price at $19, and you become an employee of mine. As an incentive to you, I give you the option to buy stock in my company. By option, I mean that you don't have to buy it right away. In fact, I will give you up to ten years to buy the stock—at the fine price of $19, regardless of what the stock is worth when you decide to buy.

Now (and here's the trick), if the stock happens to rise over the course of about seven years to, let's say, $66, you may say to yourself, "Self, it would be good to take Bruce up on his offer to sell me shares in his company, at the great price of $19."

And (here's the real gag) you buy the stock at $19 and then immediately sell it on the stock market at the current value of $66.

You just made a profit of $47. Per share. So if my original offer was for you to buy three thousand (yes, three thousand) shares, then your profit is $141,000.

It is standard operating procedure to issue stock options to senior management, but when I worked at Wyeth, those stock options came pretty far down the food chain—as far down as me, a lowly senior manager. As *BusinessWeek* explained in 1999:

> Some companies have started giving stock options to mailroom clerks. The Watson Wyatt study found that about 19% of all employees were eligible for stock options this year, up from 12% last year. The average lowest salary for employees eligible for options was $58,000. Some companies try to argue that options grants for lower-level employees are purely extras that don't displace raises or cash bonuses. Obviously, though, any compensation that's given in options could have been given in the form of a raise or bonus. To that extent, the options are displacing traditional types of pay.[87]

And of course, I started my tenure at Wyeth when their stock was

---

87   Peter Coy, "The Problems with Stock Options," *BusinessWeek*, November 16, 1999, http://www.businessweek.com/bwdaily/dnflash/nov1999/nf91116c.htm.

at its peak of $66, and when I quit Wyeth three years later, the shares had dropped to around $40. My stock options went "underwater." Just in case you don't understand, you only make money if the stock price goes *up* from what the stock option was valued at when you were given the options. The *BusinessWeek* article continues:

> The problem with options is that the typical mid-level or junior executive cannot singlehandedly affect the price of her company's stock. She could slack off and get a windfall from a rising stock price—or work like crazy and be penalized by a plunge in the stock.[88]

But one of the directors I knew, let's call him Wyeth Guy, cashed in stock options at the $66 peak that were given to him when the stock was—wait for it—at $19.

I don't know how many options he cashed in, but needless to say he had that greedy/guilty look that cats get on their face when they bring home a dead bird and lay it at your feet by the coffee table.

Wyeth is a big company. So how many other employees cashed in their options at the peak? Theoretically, let's say there were ninety-nine other employees who had been around as long as Wyeth Guy, and it would be safe to say that some of them were higher up in management, so likely to have been offered more than, as per my example, three thousand shares; but for the sake of this lesson, let's use three thousand shares (to keep the math easy), multiplied by a hundred employees:

3000 x 100 x (66-19) = $14,100,000.

Let's write that one out, too: Fourteen million, one hundred thousand dollars and zero cents.

So here's Wyeth, running a successful company despite a $20 billion litigation suit (but they are self-insured, so that didn't matter), and suddenly people are selling stock and taking 14 million dollars out of the value of the shares and the company. Where does that money come from? Is it a coincidence that the stock suddenly plummeted? They will tell you, and Wall Street will tell you, that the catalyst for the stock plummeting was the FDA announcement about a published report on hormone therapy leading to an increased risk of breast cancer.

Now let's see, if I recall what I said back in Chapter 8, Nortel's

---

88 Ibid.

stock plummeted on the announcement that they missed their targets, and it was also the dot-com bubble bursting, but at the same time, John Roth was busy cashing in his $135 million in stock options. Coincidence?

There was a time when companies were not required to keep track of what they had floating out there in stock options. The presumption was that if someone was going to cash in their options, the company must be doing well, so there was a lot of money to go around.

The issue here is something called "stock dilution." That is, when large amounts of stock options are cashed in, suddenly this large amount of stock enters the financial arena, seemingly out of nowhere, and this usually leads to a decline in the stock price. Asks *Trading Stocks Guide*:

> Who *really* pays for the employees then when a company decides to issue stock options? The existing shareholders do when they have their ownership in the company reduced. I am not implying that stock options are bad—when a company can increase its profitability at a rate greater than the dilution, then generally speaking the dilution is acceptable by the shareholders. However, when options are issued rapidly beyond prudence, the shareholders suffer badly.[89]

The battle has been on since the early '90s to get companies to account for their stock options, because in reality, the $14,100,000 or the $135,000,000 that I have used in my examples was at one time money that belonged to the shareholders.

This has finally changed. In 2004 and 2005, rules were implemented so that a fair-value assessment of the amount of outstanding stock options was reflected in the bottom line of the company.

With options strewn about like rice at a wedding and ways to manipulate a company's books so as to make the stock go up—such as cost-cutting to meet the forecasts—it is in the best interest of the

---

89 "Stock Dilution," *Trading Stocks Guide*, accessed March 19, 2009, http://www.tradingstocksguide.com/investing-stocks/stock-dilution.php. Used by permission.

senior management, and especially the CEOs, to do whatever they can to get the stock to go up.

So what is the difference between a company that doesn't tie senior management's compensation to stock options versus one that does? According to that 1999 *BusinessWeek* article:

> Heavy use of stock options seems to make top execs adopt overly risky strategies, some studies suggest. And options seem to make lower-level employees feel as if their compensation—so dependent on the performance of their company's stock—has been divorced from their own job performance.
>
> Sanders found that overall compensation was highest, and performance was worst, among companies that grant lots of options and don't tie cash compensation closely to past performance. Conversely, the best performance came from CEOs who got relatively few options and had lots of their cash compensation tied to past performance.
>
> Sanders found that CEOs whose pay is tied up in options are more likely to make lots of acquisitions. His theory: Of all the things a company can do with its money, acquisitions are among the riskiest. If you hold a lot of options that are "out of the money"—that is, not worth exercising at the current stock price—you will be richly rewarded if your acquisition bet pays off. The stock will soar above your options' exercise price, and you can cash in. On the other hand, if the acquisition fails, the stock crashes, and your options become worthless, so what? Your options were out of the money to start with, so it's no great loss.

> It turned out that the executive pay of the worst acquirers was five times more reliant on stock options than the pay of the best acquirers. Another study by Richard DeFusco of the University of Nebraska in 1991 found that the volatility of a company's stock tended to increase after it adopted a stock-option plan."[90]

So, in fact, studies show that the company is at greater risk and the stock is more volatile when stock options can reap big benefits for senior management. But some people think this is a good thing. The *BusinessWeek* article continues:

> Defenders of options say the risk-engendering nature of options is actually a good thing for shareholders.
>
> The reason: Most shareholders have a well-diversified portfolio, so they're happy if the managers of the companies they own take some risks in pursuit of big rewards.[91]

I wonder if the "defenders of options" are the same people who stand to make the most from them?

> The research is showing that stock options don't live up to their promise. They don't motivate executives and lower-level employees to do the right thing for shareholders. And if they don't do that, then what, really, is the whole point?[92]

Here, in a 2002 article, the *Graziado Business Review* rounds up some famous names from the past and their ethics when it comes to stock-price manipulation:

---

90 Peter Coy, "The Problems with Stock Options," *BusinessWeek*, November 16, 1999, http://www.businessweek.com/bwdaily/dnflash/nov1999/nf91116c.htm.
91 Ibid.
92 Ibid.

Companies such as Enron, Global Crossing, and WorldCom used accounting treatments that were improper and unethical in order to inflate net income and earnings per share. These company executives were motivated to increase the stock price because it would be financially rewarding to the management since they held substantial options on the stock. If the companies had been required to record an expense at the time the option was granted, they would not have been so generous with the options. By curtailing the options, the incentive to inflate net income and earning per share would have been reduced.[93]

Let's look again at a fantastic line from that quote: "These company executives were motivated to increase the stock price because it would be financially rewarding to the management since they held substantial options on the stock." If being motivated really means—based on what we now know of the aforementioned companies—to be lying, cheating, and stealing (to be polite), or perhaps being criminal masterminds (to be truthful), then those methods may fall from favor once a few of their peers get busted.

There is another approach to gaining big through stock options in a more direct, illegal, and sometimes difficult-to-detect method. You could falsify documents to make it look like you were granted the options at a time when the stock was lower than it actually is. From a 2006 CNET News report:

> Apple Computer's stock took a hit early Wednesday after a report that company executives had made up details on stock option administration documents to guarantee profits for certain executives.
>
> Apple is one of many companies—including CNET Networks, publisher of CNET News.com—embroiled

---

93 Charles J. McPeak, "Consider the Pros and Cons of Expensing Stock Options—Thinking Twice about FASB's Proposed Standard," *Graziado Business Review* Volume 5, Issue 4 (2002), accessed March 21, 2009, http://gbr.pepperdine.edu/024/options.html.

in government investigations into the practice of stock option backdating, in which companies would assign favorable grant dates to stock options in order to ensure hefty profits for executives.

The report said falsified documents were unearthed by Apple's internal probe into the matter. Earlier this year, Apple said it had identified concerns with two former executives as a result of its investigation into its accounting for stock options ... although it's unclear whether they are the ones thought to have falsified the documents.[94]

So if members of senior management are eyeing what they can do to make the stock go up so they can cash out big time, then it's likely they do not have your best interests at heart. As Jacque Fresco says in the movie *Zeitgeist: Addendum*:

Whether it is dumping toxic waste, having a monopoly enterprise, or downsizing the workforce, the motive is the same: profit. They are all different degrees of the same self-preserving mechanism, which always puts the well-being of people second to the monetary gain. Therefore, corruption is not some byproduct of monetary-ism, it is the very foundation ... So when you say industry cares for people, that's not true. They can't afford to be ethical. So your system is not designed to serve the well-being of people. If you still don't understand that, there would be no outsourcing of jobs if they cared about people. Industry does not care about people. They only hire people because it hasn't been automated yet. So don't talk about decency and ethics. We cannot afford it and remain in business.[95]

---

94 Tom Krazit, "Report: Apple Executives Faked Stock Option Documents," CNET News, December 27, 2006, http://news.cnet.com/2100-1014_3-6146011.html.
95 Peter Joseph, "An interview with Jacque Fresco," *Zeitgeist: Addendum*, (GMP 2008), http://vimeo.com/13770061.

Who do you have your stocks invested with? What is their strategy for increasing their stock price? What are their ethics? Are you feeling comfortable? Do you feel like leaving your money under the Christmas tree? As the *Graziado Business Review* article points out:

> It is difficult to believe that the management or the Board of Directors of Enron would have limited the number of options simply because of the requirement to record an expense. Management that is truly unscrupulous is concerned strictly about personal gain and not about the company's income statement.[96]

Okay. So outside of the Enrons and WorldComs, there are lots of companies that wouldn't do this, correct? Don't be so sure, says CNET News:

> Some companies have independently confirmed that they've been contacted by federal investigators. Those include Altera, Applied Micro Circuits, Asyst Technologies, CNET Networks (publisher of CNET News.com), Equinix, Foundry Networks, Intuit, Marvell Technology Group, RSA Security and VeriSign. In addition, other companies, such as Apple Computer and The Cheesecake Factory have announced their own, preemptive investigations.[97]

Everybody's doing it! Why can't I? How widespread is the practice of backdating?

Erik Lie, a finance professor at the University of Iowa's College of Business, has evaluated thousands of option grants and found that it was statistically improbable for them not to have been backdated at many companies:

---

96 Charles J. McPeak, "Consider the Pros and Cons of Expensing Stock Options—Thinking Twice about FASB's Proposed Standard," *Graziado Business Review* Volume 5, Issue 4 (2002), last accessed March 21, 2009, http://gbr.pepperdine.edu/024/options.html.

97 Declan McCullagh, Erik Lie, and Randall Heron, "FAQ: Behind the Stock Options Uproar," CNET News, July 26, 2006, http://news.cnet.com/FAQ-Behind-the-stock-options-uproar/2100-1014_3-6098457.html.

A paper that Lie and Randall Heron, an associate professor at Indiana University's business school, published on July 14 estimates that 18.9 percent of unscheduled grants to top executives from 1996 through 2005 were backdated or manipulated. The pair estimates that 29.2 percent of firms manipulated grants to top executives at some point between 1996 and 2005.[98]

That 29.2 percent represents just under a third of all firms. That could be perceived to be a lot. I don't know about you, but in my world, this is frightening!

And how about a little Canadian content? It seems our Canadian darlings, Research in Motion (RIM), the makers of your BlackBerry, couldn't keep their fingers out of the pie either. This report is from the January 22, 2009 edition of Canada's national newspaper, the *Globe and Mail*:

> The Ontario Securities Commission is seeking a record penalty—one that could be as high as $100-million—from the top two executives of Research In Motion Ltd. to pay for their role in a stock option accounting controversy dating back to 1996.
>
> According to people familiar with settlement discussions, the OSC's staff is in advanced discussions with lawyers representing RIM's co-chief executive officers, Jim Balsillie and Mike Lazaridis. The OSC's investigation began in 2006 and sources said the regulator began negotiating a potential settlement last fall.
>
> It is understood that the OSC has pushed for Mr. Balsillie to pay the bulk of any penalty and relinquish his seat on RIM's board of directors for a period of time. Although one person familiar with the talks said the parties are nearing a potential agreement,

---

98 Ibid.

nothing has been finalized, including how much each executive may have to pay.

In 2007, a special committee of RIM's board investigated the back-dating issue, and determined the company had backdated more than 40 per cent of stock options granted to employees since 1996. It also concluded that 12 of the 16 option grants made to Mr. Balsillie and Mr. Lazaridis between 1996 and 2006, to acquire a total of two million shares, were priced using an incorrect date.

The committee estimated the value of benefit to the two men was about $1.6-million (U.S.) each, gains that they have already repaid, along with full legal costs, to the company.

Before the release of the report, RIM notified the U.S. Securities and Exchange Commission and the OSC that it had uncovered evidence of backdating.

If a full $100-million penalty were approved, it would rank as the largest penalty paid by individuals to the OSC. The largest individual payment ever made to the OSC came from former Laidlaw Inc. chief executive officer Michael DeGroote, who agreed to pay $23-million in 1993 to settle allegations of illegal insider trading.

Mr. Balsillie and Mr. Lazaridis have been hailed as technology and business visionaries for revolutionizing wireless communications with the introduction of RIM's BlackBerry in 1999. The popular BlackBerry transformed the company into one of Canada's biggest global success stories.

The RIM board review occurred at a time when U.S. regulators were unveiling a flurry of investigations of major U.S. companies for stock option backdating. Many companies announced voluntary reviews of their past option practices as the SEC signaled it would treat companies more favorably if they came forward voluntarily.

The U.S. Securities and Exchange Commission investigated more than 100 companies over allegations of stock options backdating, including Apple Inc. It reached several backdating settlements, the largest coming in 2007 with a $468-million payment from former executives of United Health Group Inc.

Stock options give company employees the right to buy shares at a set price - typically the price at the end of the trading session on the date a grant is made. Backdating happens when companies set the grant date retroactively to align with a stock's low point, creating an instant paper gain.

According to the RIM special committee report, all option grants, except those to the company's co-CEOs, were made by or under the authority of Mr. Balsillie "including grants that have been found to have been accounted for incorrectly."

The company subsequently restated its financial statements back to 1999, recording a $248-million (U.S.) after-tax expense related to improper accounting over a variety of option granting issues.

The initial report, issued in March, 2007, also included a statement that the special committee "did not find intentional misconduct on the part of any director, officer or employee responsible for the administration of the company's stock option grant program."

At the time the special committee report was released, RIM said all employees and executives agreed to repay any benefit they received from options that were incorrectly priced. Mr. Balsillie and Mr. Lazaridis additionally agreed to pay $5-million (Canadian) each to defray the company's costs of its investigation and financial restatement.

The two men later agreed to pay an additional $2.5-million (Canadian) each to the company to compensate it for its investigation costs as part of a settlement RIM reached in a class-action lawsuit brought by Canadian shareholders over the option backdating. The settlement included no admission of wrongdoing.

RIM also announced in March, 2007, that Mr. Balsillie would step down as RIM's chairman, but remain co-CEO and a director on the board. Two long-serving directors also agreed to resign and two new directors were appointed: Royal Bank of Canada chief operating officer Barbara Stymiest and IBM Canada chief executive officer John Wetmore.[99]

Jim Balsillie is the guy who once tried to buy the Phoenix Coyotes and move that NHL hockey team to Hamilton, Ontario—my hometown. No wonder the NHL didn't want to do business with him. The RIM execs ended up paying nearly CDN$77 million to the Ontario Securities Commission, but they didn't go to jail. If we had

---

99 Jacquie McNish, Janet McFarland, and Paul Waldie, "Securities Watchdog Pursues Record Fine for RIM Execs," *Globe and Mail*, January 22, 2009, http://www.theglobeandmail.com/report-on-business/article967898.ece. Used with permission of The Globe and Mail, © CTVglobemedia Publishing Inc. All rights reserved.

caught the RIM executives digging a tunnel into Fort Knox, would they go unpunished? But of course, if we had caught some out-of-work, down-on-their-luck people digging the tunnel, they would be locked up and throw away the key.

In all cases, they were in the process of attempting to pull off a heist (which is in itself a crime). And I use Fort Knox as the example because the RIM executives were trying to pull off a theft of major proportions. These millionaires are trying to cart off millions and millions of dollars that are supposed to be shared with the shareholders! I had a cousin who once deposited a forty-dollar check into an automated teller and then immediately withdrew the funds (the check was bogus, but he needed the money), and he got a criminal record for that—a forty-dollar fraud.

So why would these greedy millionaires attempt this? They know that the punishment does not fit the crime. Conrad Black got caught taking millions that were supposed to be shared with his shareholders, and he got sentenced to six and a half years in prison. And what about Martha Stewart? Five months in prison for obstructing a federal securities investigation. Why didn't the RIM execs go to jail? I still haven't caved in to getting a BlackBerry, but I did finally get a smartphone.

Here, from a 2009 *Financial Times* article, is a fascinating diatribe on the difference between the savings-and-loans scandal of the late '80s and our current financial crisis:

> How many financiers do you think ended up in jail after America's Savings and Loans scandals? The answer can be found in a fascinating, old report from the US Department of Justice. According to some of its records, between 1990 and 1995 no less than 1,852 S&L officials were prosecuted, and 1,072 placed behind bars. Another 2,558 bankers were also jailed, often for offenses which were S&L-linked too.
>
> Those are thought-provoking numbers. These days the Western world is reeling from another massive financial crisis, that eclipses the S&L debacle in terms of wealth destruction. Yet, thus far, very few prison

terms have been handed out. For sure, there have been a few high-profile dramas. Bernie Madoff is one, obvious, example. But one reason why the Madoff drama has grabbed so much attention and already sparked a slew of books this month, is precisely because there are precious few other financiers behind bars, or facing momentous fines. Compared to the S&L days, the level of retribution so far seems almost non-existent ... Yet, in private many lawyers, and some government officials too, seem pretty cynical about just how many jail sentences or fines these initiatives will produce. In part that is because of the sheer complexity of the financial deals in the recent crisis, and the fact that these deals were often deliberately and cleverly constructed to "arbitrage" the law (i.e. skirt, but not break it).... But, on the other hand, if there is no retribution against financiers, it will be very difficult to force a real change in behavior. After all, no amount of twiddling with Basel rules or pious statements about bonuses will ever scare a financier as much as the thought of jail.

Moreover, without some retribution it will also be hard to persuade voters that finance is really being reformed, or has any credibility or moral authority. That is bad for politicians and regulators. However, it is also bad for bankers too. So, in the months ahead, keep a close eye on what happens to the legal cases in the system and, above all, watch to see just how many do (or do not) quietly die, compared to those S&L days.[100]

And speaking of people not going to jail, what about those crazy banks who are laundering money for the drug cartels and laundering money for the foreign countries that are under trade sanctions and when caught, only have to pay a fine—no one goes to jail!

Barclays was fined $298 million for laundering money for Cuba, Iran, Libya, Myanmar, and Sudan.

ABN Amro Bank was fined $500 million, and Credit Suisse Group was fined $560 million for laundering money for Iran, Libya, and Sudan.

Union Bank of California, American Express Bank International, BankAtlantic, and Wachovia have all admitted criminal conduct for laundering of money for drug cartels, and paid the government a cut of their—or is it the drug cartel's—profits. I think in diamond terms, this is called "blood money."[101] In all of these cases, *nobody went to jail.* This is absurd!

As the American judicial system is not really set up to deal with complex financial criminal dealings, these cases prove difficult to prosecute. From *American News Project*:

> Criminal fraud may be the most underreported aspect of our current financial crisis.... Former subprime lenders from Ameriquest, once the country's largest lender, describe a system rife with fraud. They describe how a "by-any-means-necessary" policy rushed employees to cut corners and falsify documents on bad mortgages and then sell the toxic assets to Wall Street banks eager to make fast profits.[102]

---

100 Gillian Tett, "Insight: A Matter of Retribution," *Financial Times*, September 3, 2009, http://us.ft.com/ftgateway/superpage.ft?news_id=fto090320091244573891. Used with permission of The Financial Times Copyright © 2010. All rights reserved.
101 Robert Mazur, "Follow the Dirty Money," *New York Times,* September 13, 2010, http://www.nytimes.com/2010/09/13/opinion/13mazur.html.
102 Lagan Sebert, "Road to Ruin: Mortgage Fraud Scandal Brewing," *American News Project*, May 11, 2009, http://americannewsproject.com/videos/road-ruin-mortgage-fraud-scandal-brewing.

I encourage you to go to the Americannewsproject.com link and watch the video that accompanies that text.

You may read or hear about executives cashing in their stock options, but how often do you hear just how much they pocketed by doing so? One more real-world example from my friends at Pfizer and Wyeth, from *Philly.com*:

> In a 348-page filing with the Securities and Exchange Commission, Pfizer detailed the months of pursuit until the $68 billion buyout offer [of Wyeth] was approved Jan. 25.
>
> The SEC filing details the multimillion-dollar deals that Wyeth senior executives will receive in stock, stock options, cash incentive bonuses, and severance if they leave the new company.
>
> Wyeth's chief executive, Bernard Poussot, will receive $18.5 million in stock options and stock holdings, $10.2 million in a cash incentive payment, and $24.3 million in severance if the deal closes and he steps down.
>
> Wyeth chief financial officer Gregory Norden will garner $4.9 million from stock and stock options, $3 million in a cash incentive bonus, and $14.4 million in severance.
>
> Joseph M. Mahady, president of Wyeth Pharmaceuticals, will get $5.1 million from his stock and options, $3.6 million in an incentive bonus, and $11.7 million in severance.

> Wyeth chief general counsel Lawrence V. Stein will receive $4.3 million from stock holdings and options, $2.1 million in a bonus incentive, and $8 million in severance.
>
> Pfizer did not disclose what jobs will be cut, or how many of Wyeth's 47,000 employees, including 5,000 in Collegeville and Malvern, may lose their jobs.[103]

That's a lot of stock options. And that's in trade for how many job losses? *The Scientist adds it up:*

> Pfizer's $68 billion merger with Wyeth ... will mean the loss of almost 20,000 jobs ...[104]

That's a lot of job losses. Absurd.

---

103 Linda Loyd, "Pfizer Details Wyeth Deal," *Philly.com*, accessed March 28, 2009, http://www.philly.com/philly/business/20090328_Pfizer_details_Wyeth_deal.html. Used with permission of *Philadelphia Inquirer*. Copyright © 2010. All rights reserved.
104 Alla Katsnelson, "Research Loss in Pfizer-Wyeth deal," *The Scientist*, October 16, 2009, http://www.the-scientist.com/blog/display/56063/.

Chapter 12
"The Root of All Evil"

It's legal [short selling]. Just because you rob the grave doesn't mean you killed the guy.

—Samantha Bee, *The Daily Show*, March 16, 2009[105]

Technically, I cannot say that there is anything wrong with short selling. It serves a purpose that is slightly above my level of comprehension. Here is the theory, as explained by *MarketWatch*:

> They are known as buyers and sellers of last resort when liquidity tightens. If they anticipate lots of selling, they'll short the stock in question ahead of time as a hedge to protect themselves when the sell orders come in and they have to step in and buy the stock. Some investors argue short sellers keep corporate management teams honest, shining light on possible accounting gimmicks or undisclosed business problems.[106]

---

105 Samantha Bee, *The Daily Show*, Comedy Central, March 16, 2009.
106 Matt Andrejczak, "SEC Bashed over Short-Selling Ban," *MarketWatch*, September 19, 2008, http://www.marketwatch.com/news/story/sec-bashed-over-short-selling-ban/story.aspx?guid={FDC364F7-7BBF-4F48-A66C-01572807D287}&dist=hpts.

The real problem with short selling—in my humble, uneducated opinion—is the loophole that allows the people who want to take your money out from under the Christmas tree to do so in dubious but not yet indictable ways. This is what makes short selling the root of all evil as it applies to the stability of the stock market and the likelihood of you losing your investment dollars.

What is short selling? This is not something done by the likes of you and me. This is where major-league investors will take a loan from a brokerage firm in the form of stocks of a company instead of cash. It is expected that the loan will be paid back with interest. This all seems legit so far. But the key to short selling is that this major-league investor is taking a bet—a bet that the price of the stock will fall while he has it in his possession. The major-league investor sells the shares that he was loaned and bets that before he has to pay the loan back, the price of the stock will drop—so that he only has to pay back the quantity of the shares he borrowed, not the share value.

There are battles being fought on the Internet and on television as to the ethics of short selling, reaching celebrity status. Financial experts are disagreeing with each other over whether short selling is good or bad for the stock market. But again, not all aspects of short selling are bad—just the one aspect that has the dubious loophole. There is a pending lawsuit against a group of hedge funds in the US by a Canadian company that had been shorted in this "dubious" manner between 2003 and 2006.[107]

Daily Show reporter Samantha Bee (a fellow Canadian) did an exposé on short selling. Here is a transcript from the March 16, 2009, episode of a conversation that Samantha had with Andrew Horowitz, a Certified Financial Planner. Horowitz explains how short selling works:

> **Andrew Horowitz**: You actually don't own the stock; you borrow the stock from somewhere. You sell it, and then when it goes down, you buy it back. I want to give you an example. So there was a company about a year and a half ago that made these rubber shoes that were all bright colors. We'll say it was a hypothetical

---

[107] Alec Scott, "The $2-Billion Man," *Toronto Life*, originally published April 2009, http://www.torontolife.com/features/2-billion-man/.

company. And everybody had this major love affair with them, so you know what? We shorted them and did really well. The stock tanked—straight down. It goes down $50 a share within days.

Samantha Bee: What happened to the hypothetical people who worked there?

Andrew Horowitz: Well, I think probably a lot of them have been laid off, unfortunately.

Samantha Bee: Oh my God, you must have made a bundle.

Andrew Horowitz: It was very nice. At the end of the day, it's the bottom line; it's cash—it's moola; anything else is—what's the point?[108]

To be clear, this involves "borrowing" someone else's stock, selling the stock, hoping that the price of the stock goes down, buying the stock back at a lower price when the price drops, and giving the now cheaper stock back to whoever you borrowed it from, worth much less. And you get to keep the profit between what you sold it for and what you bought it back at, minus fees and commissions.

Let's look at a hypothetical math example. I take a loan of one thousand shares from you, and the stock is worth $100 per share. I then sell those shares immediately, and get 1,000 x $100 = $100,000.

Now admittedly, this is not my money, because they're your shares. But (and here is the scam) I then hire a journalist (or several journalists) and brief them on what I see wrong with the company. They go out and write about how the company is mismanaged or going to miss its forecasts or not going to bring its new electronic product to market on time. These respected journalists create fear in the investors, the media, and the public—and low and behold, the stock drops to $50 per share.

---

[108] Andrew Horowitz, interview by Samantha Bee, *The Daily Show*, Comedy Central, March 16, 2009.

I immediately buy back the thousand shares that I owe you at $50 each, and I pay you back the thousand shares that you loaned me.

I know that you are a good person; you follow the trade papers, and you read what these journalists wrote, and you agree that the company was a risk, and I give you back your shares, and you accept that it was a bad investment on your part, and now you just have to hope that the company can turn it around and the stock will go up. Except for the fact that, in this whole process, I just made a profit of $50,000. And that was only getting a loan for 1,000 shares. What if the loan had been 100,000 shares? Absurd! I hope you're good at math.

There is a chance that whoever I borrowed the shares from might be in on the scam, thus explaining why they would want to "lend" shares and then see the value fall in the first place. Not everybody is so in love with short selling. Patrick Byrne, CEO of Overstock.com, said on that March 16, 2009, *Daily Show* episode:

> Abusive short selling drives down stock prices; destroys companies; costs millions of jobs; almost destroyed our company. They get journalists to come and do hatchet jobs on them and destroy the companies for profit. It's not the American way to destroy companies.[109]

Patrick Byrne has been under fire for his opinion that short selling is bad for the financial markets. But it seems only now that the tide might be shifting for others to agree that he isn't that far off the mark. From the SEC website:

> Washington, D.C., Sept. 19, 2008 — The Securities and Exchange Commission, acting in concert with the U.K. Financial Services Authority, took temporary emergency action to prohibit short selling in financial companies to protect the integrity and quality of the securities market and *strengthen investor confidence* [emphasis is mine]. The U.K. FSA took similar action yesterday.

---

109 Patrick Byrne, interview by Samantha Bee, *The Daily Show*, Comedy Central, March 16, 2009.

The Commission's action will apply to the securities of 799 financial companies. The action is immediately effective.

SEC Chairman Christopher Cox said, "The Commission is

... committed to using every weapon in its arsenal to combat market manipulation that threatens investors and capital markets. The emergency order temporarily banning short selling of financial stocks will restore equilibrium to markets.

This action, which would not be necessary in a well-functioning market, is temporary in nature and part of the comprehensive set of steps being taken by the Federal Reserve, the Treasury, and the Congress."

This decisive SEC action calls a time-out to aggressive short selling in financial institution stocks, because of the essential link between their stock price and confidence in the institution. The Commission will continue to consider measures to address short selling concerns in other publicly traded companies.

Under normal market conditions, short selling contributes to price efficiency and adds liquidity to the markets. At present, it appears that unbridled short selling is contributing to the recent, sudden price declines in the securities of financial institutions unrelated to true price valuation. Financial institutions are particularly vulnerable to this crisis of confidence and panic selling because they depend on the confidence of their trading counterparties in the conduct of their core business.[110]

---

110 "SEC Halts Short Selling of Financial Stocks to Protect Investors and Markets," U.S. Securities and Exchange Commission, September 19, 2008, http://www.sec.gov/news/press/2008/2008-211.htm.

Call me crazy, but here's what I perceive as the contradictory comments from the SEC (which, from what we've heard so far, are not uncommon or unlikely). If it says:

> Under normal market conditions, short selling contributes to price efficiency and adds liquidity to the markets.

Then it makes me wonder why they would say they are:

> ... committed to using every weapon in its arsenal to combat market manipulation that threatens investors and capital markets. The emergency order temporarily banning short selling of financial stocks will restore equilibrium to markets.

Absurd. Perhaps the real problem is that the short-selling market manipulation just never made it to the radar, as expressed earlier by Patrick Byrne, the CEO of Overstock.com. It raises the question of who decided that short selling "... contributes to price efficiency and adds liquidity to the markets."

The financial world changed when a man named Larry Summers (you might have heard of him) went before Congress in 1999. From a March 2009 report in the *Huffington Post*:

> As Treasury Secretary under Clinton, Summers played an important role in convincing Congress in 1999 to pass the Gramm-Leach-Bliley Act, which repealed key portions of the Glass-Steagall Act and allowed commercial banks to get into the mortgage-backed securities and collateralized debt obligations game. The measure also created an oversight disaster, with supervision of banking conglomerates split among a host of different government agencies—agencies that often failed to let each other know what they were doing and what they were uncovering.

At the signing of the bill, Summers hailed it as "a major step forward to the 21st Century."

Summers also backed Phil Gramm's other financial time bomb, the Commodity Futures Modernization Act, which allowed financial derivatives to be traded without any oversight or regulation.

Indeed, during a 1998 Senate hearing, Summers testified against the regulation of the derivatives market on the grounds that we could trust Wall Street.[111]

See Appendix A for Larry's complete and interesting (if a little long-winded) speech during a 1998 Senate hearing, in which he makes a case for the deregulation and/or letting up of controls on the financial markets. This was referenced at the end of Chapter 7 in the interview with President Bill Clinton.

As of this writing in the fall of 2010, Larry Summers is about to step down as the director of the White House National Economic Council, the council created by President Obama to solve the financial crisis that we see may have been caused by—yes, Larry Summers! Although, according to ABC News:

> Clinton's office called to say the former president sees former Federal Reserve Chair Alan Greenspan as the one who mainly led the charge against regulating derivatives.[112]

There are accusations on the Internet by some who claim that short selling is actually the product of a very organized criminal element with ties to organized crime, the dark side of the SEC, various high- (and

---

111 Arianna Huffington, "Larry Summers: Brilliant Mind, Toxic Ideas," *Huffington Post*, March 25, 2009, http://www.huffingtonpost.com/arianna-huffington/larry-summers-brilliant-m_b_178956.html.
112 Jake Tapper, "Clinton: I Was Wrong to Listen to Wrong Advice Against Regulating Derivatives," *Political Punch* (blog), ABC News, April 17, 2010, http://blogs.abcnews.com/politicalpunch/2010/04/. Used with permission of ABC News, Program Copyright © 2010. All rights reserved.

low-) profile Wall Street trading companies and investment firms, hedge-fund managers, journalists, and just about anybody who is in on the scam to short companies through any means possible to take your money out from under the Christmas tree.[113]

There are laws against "manipulating" to achieve success through short selling, but it is my understanding that no one has ever been prosecuted.[114]

Owen A. Lamont, a professor of finance at the Yale School of Management, and co-author Jeremy C. Stein, a professor of economics at Harvard University, former senior adviser to the secretary of the treasury, and op-ed contributor to the *New York Times*, wrote in 2004 in their paper titled "Aggregate Short Interest and Market Valuations" that "… short-selling does not play a particularly helpful role in stabilizing the overall stock market."[115]

And then there is the problem of "naked" short selling. Naked short selling is when sellers do not even borrow the shares. It seems this is another legal loophole that allows people "in the know" to keep taking our millions or trillions out of the stock market and have enough clout to make the regulators think that it is important to allow them to keep doing this. From BBC News, July 27, 2009:

> However, some analysts in the securities industry warn that the new regulation on naked short-selling could have negative consequences, such as wilder price swings and market turbulence.[116]

Absurd. These seedy analysts don't want the rules changed because they are getting filthy rich from it!

How do you go about getting the rules changed? With the AIG

---

113 Deep Capture, http://www.deepcapture.com/.
114 Mark Mitchell, "Manipulating Gold and Silver: A Criminal Naked Short Position that Could Wreck the Economy," *Deep Capture*, April 2, 2010, http://www.deepcapture.com/manipulating-gold-and-silver-a-criminal-naked-short-position-that-could-wreck-the-economy/.
115 Owen A. Lamont and Jeremy C. Stein, "Aggregate Short Interest and Market Valuations," National Bureau of Economic Research Working Paper No. 10218, January 2004, http://www.nber.org/papers/w10218.
116 "US rules on abusive short selling," BBC News, July 27, 2009, http://news.bbc.co.uk/2/hi/business/8171667.stm.

debacle, Matt Taibbi wrote in Rolling Stone that one of the key turning points came early in the game when regulators were convinced by a group of investors from JP Morgan that:

> ... if they bought CDS protection for enough of the investments in their portfolio, they had effectively moved the risk off their books. Therefore, they argued, they should be allowed to lend more, without keeping more cash in reserve. A whole host of regulators—from the Federal Reserve to the Office of the Comptroller of the Currency—accepted the argument, and Morgan was allowed to put more money on the street.[117]

I guess the same type of argument was once made for short selling, because it seems the same thing applies here, that someone convinced the SEC it was a good thing—until it all goes wrong, of course. But the people who stand to make money from short selling don't want to see their ability to short sell stopped, as when it was halted temporarily in the panic days of 2008 as the financial crisis seemed to be spiraling out of control. From *MarketWatch*, September 19, 2008:

> The SEC drew sharp criticism for putting a stranglehold on short sellers, a move that will force hedge funds to reveal short positions. It also could sap market liquidity.
>
> Eric Newman, portfolio manager at TFS Capital, said the SEC is blaming short sellers for almost every problem in the financial markets.
>
> "This crisis is the result of risk management failures and disclosures by the investment firms and banks that are collapsing, not the actions of hedge fund managers,"

---

117 Matt Taibbi, "The Big Takeover," *Rolling Stone*, March 19, 2009, accessed March 19, 2009, http://www.rollingstone.com/politics/story/26793903/the_big_takeover/print.

said MFA President and former congressman Richard Baker.[118]

The rationale used by the fans of short selling seems seedy at best. Their rationale seems too much like a cover for their way to take our millions, if not billions and trillions, out from under the Christmas tree before you and I have a chance to get to it. I have to reflect back to my comments in Chapter 3 about having trouble understanding exactly how investing works. In *Rolling Stone*, Matt Taibbi looks at the confusion this way:

> The people who have spent their lives cloistered in this Wall Street community aren't much for sharing information with the great unwashed. Because all of this shit is complicated, because most of us mortals don't know what the hell LIBOR is or how a REIT works or how to use the word "zero coupon bond" in a sentence without sounding stupid—well, then, the people who do speak this idiotic language cannot under any circumstances be bothered to explain it to us and instead spend a lot of time rolling their eyes and asking us to trust them.[119]

Short selling is very complicated, and we are suffering from the complicated loopholes. There are a lot of people in positions of power (such as at the SEC) who can stop this absurdity, but they fall into Matt Taibbi's description above, and don't want to look the fool for suggesting that short selling be stopped. Either that, or they're on the take. So if those in the know (who are making millions) pull a "Bernie Madoff shout-out" and just keep pretending arrogance over our ignorance, then we all lose our retirement investments. Remember, these people are betting on the market to go bad, which it did, which

---

118 Matt Andrejczak, "SEC Bashed Over Short-Selling Ban," *MarketWatch*, September 19, 2008, http://www.marketwatch.com/news/story/sec-bashed-over-short-selling-ban/story.aspx?guid={FDC364F7-7BBF-4F48-A66C-01572807D287}&dist=hpts.

119 Matt Taibbi, "The Big Takeover," *Rolling Stone*, March 19, 2009, accessed March 19, 2009, http://www.rollingstone.com/politics/story/26793903/the_big_takeover/print.

implies that they are the ones who took the trillions of dollars that seem to have gone missing.

But now, a bright light. There is now some long-needed pushback. In the European Union, where some countries are on the verge of bankruptcy and short sellers are circling like vultures, some heads of state are pointing the finger at the short sellers—because, in effect, the short sellers are betting on the collapse of countries! From *guardian. co.uk*, May 20, 2010:

> German efforts to seize back control of the European debt crisis were met with snorts of derision in London. Investors could not decide whether the ban on short-selling was an ill-conceived gaffe, or a desperate piece of political posturing. But German chancellor Angela Merkel may have the last laugh.
>
> The ban applies only to speculators trying to bet against eurozone debt in Germany.
>
> At best, the move was dismissed as a political red herring, designed only to shore up domestic German support before a vote on the Greek bailout plan. At worst, many viewed it as a naive misunderstanding of how the market really functions.
>
> To an extent, the European emphasis on blaming the speculators is misplaced. Talk of a "wolfpack" of traders and credit rating agencies hunting down the weaker members of the eurozone ignores the fact that these are the same people indebted nations need to persuade to lend them more money. Attempts to prevent them from short-selling seem based on a misconception that governments can simply demand the confidence of investors.
>
> But a closer reading of what Merkel has said on the matter suggests something more significant is going on. In language more confrontational than any yet

used by European leaders, the chancellor first pointed out she wanted to "ensure that banks cannot extort the state anymore." Extortion is a strong word in any language, but reflects mounting anger over the way financial markets have emerged from the world's three-year banking crisis with an even greater hold over nation states than when they went in. The unspoken threat is that Europe's biggest economy has had enough and is preparing to take its ball away.

Lest anyone think this is an idle threat, Merkel called on Europe to "develop a process for an orderly state insolvency"—in other words work out how to let countries such as Greece, Spain and Portugal simply refuse to repay their debts. It might sound obvious to those on the outside, but this flies in the face of everything Europe has been trying to do and would set in train colossal losses for banks, pension funds and investors everywhere. There is no guarantee it would make life any easier for the Greeks either. Instead of having to bring public spending in line with tax revenues slowly, a decision to effectively turn its back on the financial markets would mean having to balance the books overnight—a huge wrench for a country already in the grips of a deep recession.

It would also explain some of the appetite for the ban on short-selling shares in German banks. If Merkel really is preparing to hit the market with a Lehman Brothers style default that would rock banks across Europe, the last thing she wants is for lots of speculators to get rich in the process. Those patronising voices in London need to remember similar measures were put in place by the Financial Services Authority and the US Securities and Exchange Commission in New York during the banking crisis. To many the notion of an "orderly insolvency" is an oxymoron, but to those who believe the global debt crisis is entering its final stage, it is perhaps the best that can be hoped for. The emphasis on "orderliness" may simply be the German way of trying to keep the eurozone together in the process.

For many investors, the French approach of pouring more and more money on the problem looks the more appealing – promising years of volatility and trading opportunities at the expense of taxpayers. A German scorched earth policy could prove a lot less attractive.[120]

A special task force of the Madrid-based International Organization of Securities Commissions is calling for greater disclosure and tighter standards on short selling.[121] This represents the first coordinated global effort to more closely monitor and regulate short selling.

Originally, the stock market was set up to help companies get much-needed capital to grow their business and offer a potential reward to investors. So how did we end up with an entire industry of short sellers making billions off of failures? So as not to make this a rhetorical question, the answer is that we have this industry exactly because they *can* make billions off of failures. Perhaps that is why we are lying in the bed we made.

But because short selling is legal, it led our short-selling friend Andrew Horowitz to say, "It is un-American not to short sell."[122]

Is that regardless of the consequences, Mr. Horowitz? The SEC was led to believe that short selling was a good thing, but in the meantime billions (if not trillions) of dollars have been sucked out of the stock market by short sellers taking advantage of the fact that, as Jim Cramer mentioned earlier, "the SEC doesn't understand it anyway."

---

120 Dan Roberts, "Germans Are Not Posturing on Short-Selling: They're Deadly Serious," *guardian.co.uk*, May 20, 2010, http://www.guardian.co.uk/business/dan-roberts-on-business-blog/2010/may/19/viewpoint-german-short-selling. Copyright Guardian News & Media Ltd., 2010.
121 "IOSCO Technical Committee Members' Initiatives Relating To Restrictions on Short Sales," International Organization of Securities Commissions, October 2, 2008, http://www.iosco.org/news/pdf/IOSCONEWS129.pdf.
122 Andrew Horowitz, interview by Samantha Bee, *The Daily Show,* Comedy Central, March 16, 2009.

When short sellers pile into a stock or a security, it creates panic selling.

—David Weidner, MarketWatch Financial Analyst
The Daily Show, March 16, 2009[123]

Essentially they buy fire insurance on the company, and then they burn it down.

—Patrick Byrne, CEO, Overstock.com
The Daily Show, March 16, 2009[124]

It's easy for anyone to justify his position if he can have a battle of wits with an unarmed person, and it seems that the SEC is unarmed. If short selling is now reaching a critical mass where more and more investors are figuring out how to do it (somewhat) legally with incredible returns, *then why would they do anything else*? Everybody wants to get in on the game.

This is what legislators never seem to take into consideration. We need statistics that show us just how much money the short sellers pull out of the market through their shorting and/or a more direct correlation between shorting a stock and the effect that shorting has on the stock price. It's all a little too loose for my liking. It seems that the entire short-selling market is poised to take our trillions out from under the Christmas tree with their bet that the world is going to go bankrupt. Absurd!

It's been said that our economy is on life support. Let's expand that analogy, as the *Wall Street Journal* does here:

> The body is trying to fight off a disease that is spreading, and as it does so, the body convulses, settles for a time and then convulses again. The illness seems to be overwhelming the self-healing tendencies of markets. The doctors in charge are resorting to ever-

---

123 David Weidner, interview by Samantha Bee, *The Daily Show*, Comedy Central, March 16, 2009.
124 Patrick Byrne, interview by Samantha Bee, *The Daily Show*, Comedy Central, March 16, 2009.

more invasive treatment, and are now experimenting with remedies that have never before been applied.[125]

Perhaps we've discovered that the disease is a mutation of the short-selling virus; the mutation has become the loophole that allows the virus to bring the patient to near death. Cure the mutation, and we might cure the disease. Just sayin'.

Let's close this chapter with a final comment from Horowitz, from his conversation with Samantha Bee on *The Daily Show*:

> **Andrew Horowitz**: Listen, nobody wants the company to go down, nobody wants bad things to happen, nobody wants layoffs, that's not part of the equation. We are not excited about the company failing necessarily, we're excited 'cause we're profiting. But you know what, if this is the law, and this is the role, I mean, somebody should profit on it.
>
> **Samantha Bee**: It's legal. Just because you rob the grave doesn't mean you killed the guy.
>
> **Andrew Horowitz**: We actually shorted the municipal bonds of Manhattan.
>
> **Samantha Bee**: You short sold Manhattan?
>
> **Andrew Horowitz**: Correct. It's been a party, it's been a party of short selling right now.[126]

Absurd. My guess is that some day we are going to discover that the level of corruption in the financial markets goes all the way to the top—of the chimney. Merry fucking Christmas.

---

125 Jon Hilsenrath, Serena Ng, and Damian Paletta, "Worst Crisis Since '30s, With No End Yet in Sight," *Wall Street Journal*, September 18, 2008, http://online.wsj.com/article/SB122169431617549947.html.

126 Andrew Horowitz, interview by Samantha Bee, *The Daily Show*, Comedy Central, March 16, 2009.

Chapter 13
"Confusion Will be My Epitaph"

> Markopolos's opus: "I've found that wherever there is one cockroach in plain sight, many more are lurking behind the corner out of plain view."[127]
>
> —*The Independent, January 29, 2009*

Paul Krugman said it in Chapter 3: "If you aren't outraged, you haven't been paying attention."[128]

During the March 9, 2009 episode of *The Daily Show*, Jon Stewart said to Jim Cramer, "These guys at these companies [who] were on a Sherman's march through their companies, financed by our 401Ks, and all the incentives of their companies were for short-term profit. And they burned the fucking house down with our money and walked away rich-as-hell, and you guys knew that that was going on."[129]

As Norman Lear said in Chapter 10, "The systemic disease that got us here [is] short-term thinking; the lunatic need for a profit statement

---

127 "The Madoff Files: Bernie's Billions," *Independent*, January 29, 2009, http://www.independent.co.uk/news/business/analysis-and-features/the-madoff-files-bernies-billions-1518939.html.

128 Paul Krugman, "Rewarding Bad Actors," *New York Times*, August 2, 2009, http://www.nytimes.com/2009/08/03/opinion/03krugman.html.

129 Jon Stewart, *The Daily Show*, Comedy Central, March 12, 2009.

this quarter considerably larger than the last, at the expense of every other value."[130]

In Chapter 7, Lawrence Mishel said, "I find it unfathomable that people are not horrified about what is going to happen."[131]

There seem to be a few good financial guiding lights out there. It's people like Harry Markopolos and Peter Schiff and Nobel prize–winning Paul Krugman who seem to want to help expose the cockroaches hiding under the fridge. And we owe many thanks to the candid observations of people like Jon Stewart of *The Daily Show* and Matt Taibbi of *Rolling Stone*. We can only hope that President Obama gets good, or perhaps better, advice to help solve the crisis.

In the meantime, I realize that this book is time sensitive, and by the time you read this, some elements may have changed ... or perhaps not. If it takes about a year to get this book from being written to being put on bookshelves, and the financial crisis is the same or worse, and unemployment is the same or worse, and the value of your stock portfolio is the same or worse, then you know that the moral of the story is that the naysayers were correct.

If gold does go up to $5,000 per ounce, then Peter Schiff was damn right. But then that would also mean that the American dollar would likely be on skid row. If the domino effect collapses more and more businesses and industries, and it looks like we're all going to hell in a hand basket, then let it be said that you were warned. Not by me. This book is just an armchair quarterback's musings. The professionals have been mentioned above and quoted extensively throughout.

Let me tell you one of the things I did with my investments. I put money into gold at the beginning of 2010, and it grew 15 percent in one year. I did some math and calculated that if I had invested in five ounces of gold each year from the time I started contributing to my retirement savings fund in the mid-'70s, my current retirement portfolio would be worth twice as much as it is now. Peter Schiff says,

---

130 Norman Lear, "Come, Shoot the Messengers!" *Huffington Post*, March 19, 2009, http://www.huffingtonpost.com/norman-lear/come-shoot-the-messengers_b_176692.html.

131 Michael A. Fletcher, "Recovery's Missing Ingredient: New Jobs," *Washington Post*, June 22, 2009, http://www.washingtonpost.com/wp-dyn/content/article/2009/06/21.

"I have long been an advocate of fortifying investment portfolios with precious metals."[132] From his website:

> Precious metals are volatile, speculative, and high-risk investments. Physical ownership will not yield income. As with all investments, an investor should carefully consider his investment objectives and risk tolerance as well as any fees and/or expenses associated with such an investment before investing. The value of the investment will fall and rise. Investing in precious metals may not be suitable for all investors.[133]

Here is a quote from 2005 where Dr. Steve Sjuggerud talks about gold but with a foreshadowing references to the current financial crisis:

> … For the masses to pile into gold, they need to believe that we are at war. And most important, they need to believe that the men at the controls are no longer in control …
>
> In January of 1980 … Gold hit $850 an ounce. After a decade of dumb ideas from our political leaders (including Nixon's price controls), the Vietnam War, and the OPEC oil embargo, we were stuck with drastic inflation, high unemployment, and no signs of economic growth …[134]

Sound familiar? Good luck with your investing—you'll need it. And I think it is only appropriate to leave the last word to the man,

---

132 Peter Schiff, "Peter Schiff's Five Favorite Gold & Silver Mining Stocks," Euro Pacific Capital Inc., last accessed November 27, 2010, http://www.europac.net/special_report/peter_schiffs_five_favorite_gold_silver_mining_stocks.
133 Peter Schiff, "Precious Metals Investment Strategies," Euro Pacific Capital Inc., last accessed November 27, 2010, http://www.europac.net/Precious_Metals_Investment_Strategies_1
134 Dr. Steve Sjuggerud, "Gold Stocks: 2 Ways To Size Up Investment Buys," *Investment U*, September 20, 2005, http://www.investmentu.com/IUEL/2005/20050920.html.

the Boss, who has spoken for the working class for forty years now, and it is apropos that he said this while a guest on *The Daily Show* with Jon Stewart:

> The country has lost its moral center … the idea of work and service to the public being a part of your work feels like its been stripped away. People drank a whole lot of their own Kool-aid. There was a subculture of people that basically brought down the country, and were in a position to do that, and everybody out there is footing the bill. And you've seen President Obama struggling to find where is the moral centre of the argument he's making right now.
>
> —*Bruce Springsteen*
> *The Daily Show, March 19, 2009*[135]

---

135 Bruce Springsteen, interview by Jon Stewart, *The Daily Show*, Comedy Central, March 19, 2009.

About the Author

On the artistic side, as a composer and musician, Bruce Gauthier has released nine CDs. Bruce's music can be heard streaming at http://bruce.fm

Bruce had his track "Then They Start to Wonder THEN" included on the Bill Nelson tribute CD *Several Famous Orchestras Vol. III.* As well, Bruce had his track "I'm Angry" included on *TEA (Toronto Experimental Artists) Volume III*. Bruce composed the soundtrack and narrated the film *Landfall* for Canadian filmmaker Rick Hancox. Bruce has also composed film soundtracks for Karen Saunders' *I must keep my lips together, I must keep my teeth apart*, and Phil Hoffman's *The River*. Bruce has also composed soundtracks for his own films *Repetition, Repetition* and *The Death Rate on Earth is 100%*.

On the career side of life, Bruce is a freelance technical director for corporate events, having worked in Asia, Australia, Europe, the Caribbean, and North America. For numerous production companies, Bruce has been the technical manager for the staging of private corporate concerts by Andrea Bocelli in Rome; Steve Winwood in Berlin; Keith Urban in New York City; Huey Lewis and the News in Maui; Metric, Celine Dion, and the Barenaked Ladies in Toronto; and many others.

On the financial side, Bruce became really angry at himself when he let his life savings slip away in the current financial meltdown. He began to follow closely how the press presented the state of the recession and took notes. Those notes became a form of anger management, and he focused his energy into this book.

Appendix A: Larry Summers Testimony July 1998

FROM THE OFFICE OF PUBLIC AFFAIRS

July 30, 1998
RR-2616

TREASURY DEPUTY SECRETARY LAWRENCE H. SUMMERS TESTIMONY BEFORE THE SENATE COMMITTEE ON AGRICULTURE, NUTRITION, AND FORESTRY ON THE CFTC CONCEPT RELEASE

Mr Chairman, thank you for giving me the opportunity to discuss issues raised recently regarding the regulation of the OTC derivatives market—notably, the concept release issued last May by the Commodity Futures Trading Commission ("CFTC") and the subsequent legislative proposal put forward jointly by Secretary Rubin and the Chairmen of the Federal Reserve Board and Securities and Exchange Commission ("SEC").

As you know, Mr Chairman, the CFTC's recent concept release has been a matter of serious concern, not merely to Treasury but to all those with an interest in the OTC derivatives market. In our view, the Release has cast the shadow of regulatory uncertainty over an otherwise thriving market—raising risks for the stability and competitiveness of American derivative trading. We believe it is quite important that the doubts be eliminated.

Let me devote my remarks to three aspects of this issue:

- the CFTC's concept release and the immediate risks to the American derivatives market that were posed by that release;
- the rationale for temporary legislation to allay the immediate uncertainties triggered by the release and to enable Congress to undertake careful consideration of these issues;
- some of the broader, conceptual considerations that should be taken into account when analyzing questions of the proper regulation of this market going forward.

I. Concerns Raised by the CFTC's Concept Release

Mr Chairman, the American OTC derivatives market is second to none. In a few short years it has assumed a major role in our own economy and become a magnet for derivative business from around the world. The dramatic development of this market has occurred on the basis of complex and fragile legal and legislative understandings—understandings which the CFTC release put into question.

Let me first explain the principal legal and regulatory uncertainties created by the CFTC's concept release that was made public on May 7. I will then briefly explain the potential economic and financial concerns posed by the creation of this kind of legal uncertainty.

Legal and regulatory uncertainties created by the concept release

The CFTC concept release raises important issues concerning the regulatory regime governing the OTC derivatives market. Without doubt, the CFTC release has raised legitimate questions that merit study, discussion, and debate. I will be returning to some of these longer term questions in a moment. However, by raising these questions in the manner it has, two major problems have been caused.

First, the concept release implicitly assumes that the CFTC has broad jurisdiction over the OTC derivatives market. This is far from clear. The concept release has thereby increased concern about the legal status of OTC derivatives, particularly those based on so-called non-exempt securities—that is, those securities that are not exempt from the registration provisions of the securities laws. These derivatives include some equity derivatives, emerging market security derivatives, and credit derivatives, among others.

If the CFTC did have broad jurisdiction over the OTC derivatives market, it would have to be based on a judgment that many swaps are the principal type of contract covered by the Commodities Exchange Act (CEA)—namely futures contracts. This, in turn, would call into question the legality of swaps involving non-exempt securities, because the CFTC does not have the authority to exempt futures contracts based on non-exempt securities from the exchange trading requirement of the CEA that is embedded in the Shad-Johnson Accord. Consequently, if OTC derivatives based on non-exempt securities are deemed to be futures contracts, they could be viewed as illegal and unenforceable.

Second, the concept release causes uncertainty for other types of OTC derivatives—even those that would clearly be covered by the CFTC's exemptive authority if they were deemed to be futures contracts—since it raises the possibility of increased regulation over this market.

Mr Chairman, for the past ten years, there has been an implicit consensus that the OTC derivatives market should be allowed to grow and evolve without deciding the various questions concerning the potential applicability of the CEA to any of these transactions. At the heart of that consensus has been a recognition that "swap" transactions should not be regulated as contracts subject to the CEA, whether or not a plausible legal argument could be made that any of these transactions are covered by the CEA.

The CFTC concept release, even though it purports to do no more than pose questions, upsets this fragile consensus because it suggests that the CFTC is at least considering imposing a significant new regulatory requirements on the OTC derivatives market. This, in turn, can only be based on a belief that many swaps are subject to CFTC jurisdiction as futures contracts and might appropriately be regulated as such.

As I have indicated, we do not agree with this conclusion. It is our view, and that of both the Federal Reserve and the SEC, that swaps are not futures under the CEA. Thus, the Administration proposed temporary legislation to alleviate the legal uncertainty created by the release while more permanent solutions are considered.

Potential economic and financial costs of market disruption

Mr Chairman, we believe that the uncertainties created by the release posed risks to the American OTC derivatives market. This is not a possibility to be taken lightly when one considers the critical importance of these activities to the growth and efficiency of our economy.

The OTC derivatives market is a vast, increasingly global industry. By some estimates, the market now has a notional value of around $26 trillion, with contracts of more than $4 trillion undertaken in 1997 alone. The dramatic growth of the market in recent years is testament not merely to the dynamism of modern financial markets, but to the benefits that derivatives provide for American businesses.

By helping participants manage their risk exposures better and lower their financing costs, derivatives facilitate domestic and international commerce and support a more efficient allocation of capital across the economy. They can also improve the functioning of financial markets themselves by potentially raising liquidity and narrowing the bid-asked spreads in the underlying cash markets. Thus, OTC derivatives directly and indirectly support higher investment and growth in living standards in the United States and around the world.

Any disruption to this market brings two large potential costs. First, it could inhibit the use of an important risk management tool, thus reducing the efficiency our financial markets in channeling capital to its most effective use.

Second, uncertainties of this kind threaten the position of the United States relative to other global trading centers, thereby depriving our economy of the multiple benefits which this activity affords. This concern is not hypothetical. From the opening of the Lloyds coffee shop in 17th century London to the creation of the Eurodollar market in the early 1960s, the history of world financial markets offers plentiful cases in which chance differences in location or national regulation have brought major long-term consequences that could never have been predicted at the start. The lesson is that early dominance of a fast-moving industry should not be ceded lightly—and even small regulatory changes should be considered very carefully indeed.

Our discussions with market participants suggest that derivatives business is beginning to be shifted abroad because of the legal uncertainty in the U.S. We also understand from market participants that the move to curtail U.S. derivatives business and to shift much of this business abroad could accelerate if it becomes obvious that we are unwilling to address this issue.

Let me stress that this is not simply a matter of parochial Wall Street concern. Quite apart from the potential loss of key decision-making positions in the financial services industry and a decline in the depth and liquidity of our financial market, the broader economy would be adversely affected as firms would find it more costly—impossible, even—to obtain these financial products to support their growth and investment plans.

In fact, anecdotal evidence suggests that the uncertainties created by the release had begun to spread beyond Wall Street to a broad range of industries—all of which are being deprived of an important risk management tool. For example:

- derivatives dealers who previously offered major agribusinesses with customized agriculture risk management products have reportedly begun to pull back from this line of business as a result of the current legal uncertainty;
- major U.S. corporations are reportedly delaying or reconsidering OTC derivatives transactions in their own stock that they would otherwise have used to hedge certain balance sheet risks;
- a software company developing a product to support the OTC derivatives business is said to have decided to do this business in the United Kingdom—because of a perception that the U.S. regulatory environment is inhospitable and unstable.

Mr Chairman, none of this is to suggest that markets are threatened every time that an agency reviews its regulations. The CFTC has put out numerous releases in which it has reviewed various parts of its rules with no unsettling impact on financial markets. It is only this concept release that raised such concern.

In the presence of such uncertainty about the CFTC's jurisdiction, we believe that it is up to Congress to decide whether there should be additional regulation of the OTC derivatives market in the U.S. That is why Treasury, the Federal Reserve, and the SEC have disagreed with the CFTC's actions—and the agencies jointly proposed legislation providing legal certainty, while at the same time permitting a comprehensive review of these markets and consideration of whether or not changes in the regulatory regime should be effected through legislation.

II. The Joint Treasury/Federal Reserve/SEC Proposal

Mr Chairman, the market appeared to have been somewhat reassured by the prompt expression of concern by Secretary Rubin, Chairman Greenspan, and Chairman Levitt immediately following issuance of the concept release. But market participants remain worried about what the concept release may portend. As a consequence, some business is reportedly not being done and other business is beginning to be transferred abroad.

The longer that legal uncertainty persists, the greater the risk of market problems developing and the greater the risk that the U.S. will see its leadership position in derivatives erode as market participants seek jurisdictions with more certain legal and regulatory regimes.

It was for this reason that Secretary Rubin and Chairmen Greenspan and Levitt transmitted a legislative proposal on June 5 that was designed to provide legal certainty to the market until Congress could study the issues:

- first, the proposal would temporarily prohibit the CFTC from issuing new rules regulating any swap or hybrid instrument;
- second, it would give some limited legal protection to OTC derivative instruments based on non-exempt securities; and
- third, it would require the President's Working Group to conduct a study of OTC derivatives and hybrid instruments and to report to Congress the results of this study within one year.

We understood the seriousness of making this proposal. To question an independent agency's concept of its jurisdiction and then to propose legislation that would temporarily curtail that agency's ability to act is not something we do lightly. We concluded, however, that such legislation was necessary to avoid disruption and dislocation in the market while the underlying issues were being considered by Congress.

Last Friday, Chairperson Born sent a letter to Cong. Smith, the Chairman of the House Agriculture Committee. In this letter, the CFTC agreed not to issue or propose new rules affecting swaps or hybrids until Congress reconvenes next year. It also reiterated something the CFTC had said in its 1989 Swaps Policy Statement—that "swaps are not appropriately regulated as futures." Chairman Leach described this letter as going about half of the way to a resolution. While on Monday, eight market trade associations issued a statement calling the letter a "constructive step".

We think the letter improves the situation with regard to the first two points addressed by our legislative proposal. However, as Chairman Leach noted, more needs to be done. On Monday, Chairman Smith said that it was his understanding that the CFTC would not issue or propose new rules affecting swaps or derivatives until Congress had time to consider the various issues. This is indeed welcome news, which perhaps can be amplified at today's hearing. In addition, market participants need some re-confirmation of Chairman Schapiro's statement of two years ago—that "the Commission has not taken a position on whether swap agreements are futures contracts." I believe that can be inferred from last Friday's letter, but the market would appreciate hearing it directly.

III. Longer Term Conceptual Issues Raised by Recent Debates

Even with this reassurance, Mr Chairman, there are still enormously complicated and difficult issues that Congress will have to address in next year's reauthorization. Treasury responded to the CFTC's concept release, because it poses risks to the continued strength and stability of the American OTC derivatives market. But this is not to deny that there are legitimate legal and regulatory questions involved.

As I have said, derivatives can provide important benefits to financial markets and to the economy as a whole. But clearly, they can also be abused. And there have been certain problems that have arisen in recent years in both the OTC and exchange-traded derivatives market, as well as problems arising from inappropriate investments in complex securities with embedded derivatives. More broadly, questions have been raised as to whether the derivatives markets could exacerbate a large, sudden market decline.

All of these questions merit careful study and continued vigilance. But if there is to be a broader reassessment of the regulatory and legal environment governing this market it will be important this reassessment begins from the right place—namely with the underlying rationale for government intervention in financial markets and its applicability to OTC derivatives.

Government regulation of different financial instruments in the United States has been based on one or more of the following rationales, after a demonstration of the need for additional regulation. Such rationales are first, to protect retail investors from unscrupulous traders and second, to guard against manipulation in markets where the scope for such manipulation exists. As Chairman Greenspan has noted, these have been the major concerns guiding regulation of American commodities markets from the CEA onwards.

Once again, it is legitimate and valuable for Congress to consider whether it is necessary to make changes to the regulation of the entire OTC derivatives market. But I would note that it is not immediately obvious how either of these rationales applies in the case of the vast majority of OTC derivatives:

- first, the parties to these kinds of contract are largely sophisticated financial institutions that would appear to be eminently capable of protecting themselves from fraud and counterparty insolvencies and most of which are already subject to basic safety and soundness regulation under existing banking and securities laws;

- second, given the nature of the underlying assets involved—namely supplies of financial exchange and other financial instruments—there would seem to be little scope for market manipulation of the kind seen in traditional agricultural commodities, the supply of which is inherently limited and changeable.

To date there has been no clear evidence of a need for additional regulation of the institutional OTC derivatives market, and we would submit that proponents of such regulation must bear the burden of demonstrating that need. To address problems that have arisen affecting retail investors in certain foreign currency products, we would urge enactment of the provisions to amend the CEA that Treasury proposed last year. These would give the CFTC the necessary authority to protect retail investors from unscrupulous traders without harming legitimate activity in the rest of the derivatives market.

IV. Concluding Remarks

Mr Chairman, the OTC derivatives market has grown from nothing to become a highly lucrative industry of major international importance. It is reasonable to consider whether it is necessary to make changes in how this market is regulated. But there is currently no clear consensus in the government or in the private sector concerning any possible additional regulation for this market. And there is certainly no consensus that the CFTC currently has the legal authority to regulate this market or raise questions about possible regulation of this market in the future.

In this testimony I have put forward some of the considerations that Treasury believes ought to be kept in mind in approaching a resolution of these issues going forward. But this should not distract from our basic point: that any further clarification of the situation, not to mention any new regulation of this market, ought to come with the legitimacy of a clear legislative mandate from Congress.

The CFTC's letter of last Friday does not address the third leg of the joint Treasury/Fed/SEC legislative proposal: a Working Group study of the OTC derivatives market. If legislation is not forthcoming, Secretary Rubin, as Chairman of the Working Group, has asked me to assure the Committee that the Working Group will work to assist this Committee in evaluating the issues in whatever way would be helpful. We look forward to working with this Committee, with other members of Congress and interested parties as we work to resolve these issues in a way that safeguards America's position in this fast-developing global market. Thank you. I would be happy to respond to any questions you and other members of the Committee may have.[136]

---

[136] United States Treasury Department, "Treasury Deputy Secretary Lawrence H. Summers Testimony Before the Senate Committee on Agriculture, Nutrition, and Forestry on the CFTC Concept Release—RR-2616," July 30, 1998, http://www.ustreas.gov/press/releases/rr2616.htm.

Appendix B: The Original Preface for This Book from April, 2009

In March of 2009, I got a phone call from my *supposed* financial adviser, who was calling me because he had just received the paperwork telling him that I wanted to move my funds out of his hands and into my insurance company's "cheap and cheerful" Guaranteed Income Certificates (GICs). He did rub in the fact that he normally wouldn't be dealing with someone like me who doesn't have a lot of money invested with him. I guess he was phoning because of the number of customers who were so pissed off with the performance of his funds that it was time to go elsewhere, and he was probably getting pressure from above to stop the bleeding—or maybe he was doing this because it might actually affect *his* income (although my investments wouldn't have had much of an impact).

Now, in his defense, he wouldn't have known that I was researching this book, and therefore I'd been reading as much as I could every day for the past several months with keen interest as to how the "experts" on Wall Street, with their partners in the government, were going to fix this mess.

My financial adviser told me that the only problem with my account was that I was totally in equities. He wants to move my money into "blah, blah, blah, Rover" (to paraphrase an old *Far Side* cartoon). I'm no good at understanding financial jargon, and this book tries to avoid financial prose and/or at least explain in layperson's terms exactly how the investors are going to try to take your money from you.

I decided to toy with my financial adviser a bit. I asked him what his company's position was on short selling (explained in Chapter 12 as "The Root of All Evil"). He gave me a politically correct answer.

So I told him that I wasn't going to be able to give him a second chance and would pursue my GIC option. That's when he threw the spaghetti at the wall to see what would stick. "You know, history has proven that this recession will only last a short time, and that the market is bound to come around again soon." I fired back that I thought this financial crisis was going to last a long time. And then he came out with that really pathetic phrase, "You know, I have a degree in economics. Financial models show that … blah, blah, blah, Rover."

I asked him, "How can the financial models account for the way the world has changed?" And when he replied that in economics, the model never changes, I knew then that his head was so far up his butt, like all of these "experts" on Wall Street, that there was no reason to keep the conversation going.

Bibliography

"Air Travel Trivia." *Skytrax.* Accessed September 12, 2010. http://www.airlinequality.com/main/facts.htm.

Andrejczak, Matt. "SEC Bashed Over Short-Selling Ban." *MarketWatch.* September 19, 2008. http://www.marketwatch.com/news/story/sec-bashed-over-short-selling-ban/story.aspx?guid={FDC364F7-7BBF-4F48-A66C-01572807D287}&dist=hpts.

Armstrong, Walter. "Attack of the Monster Merger." *Advanstar Communications Inc.* March 1, 2009. http://pharmexec.findpharma.com/pharmexec/article/articleDetail.jsp?id=585590&pageID=1&sk=&date=.

Bee, Samantha. *The Daily Show.* Comedy Central. March 16, 2009.

Berman, James. "Reports of the Death of Equities: Greatly Exaggerated." *Huffington Post.* March 11, 2009. http://www.huffingtonpost.com/james-berman/reports-of-the-death-of-e_b_173460.html.

Bradley, Bill. "The Crisis and How to Deal with It." *New York Review of Books.* June 11, 2009. http://www.nybooks.com/articles/22756.

Brustein, Joshua. "Obama Adviser Sees Unemployment Rising Until 2010." *New York Times.* May 10, 2009. http://www.nytimes.com/2009/05/11/business/economy/11jobs.html.

Bryne, Patrick. *The Daily Show.* Interview by Samantha Bee. Comedy Central. March 16, 2009.

Byrne, Patrick, Evren Karpak, and Mark Mitchell. *Deep Capture*. http://www.deepcapture.com/.

Cooper, Michael. "Job Loss Looms as Part of Stimulus Act Expires." *New York Times*. September 25, 2010. http://www.nytimes.com/2010/09/26/us/26stimulus.html.

Coy, Peter. "The Problems with Stock Options." *BusinessWeek*. November 16, 1999. http://www.businessweek.com/bwdaily/dnflash/nov1999/nf91116c.htm.

Cramer, Jim. *The Daily Show*. Interview by Jon Stewart. Comedy Central. March 12, 2009.

da Costa, Pedro Nicolaci, and Juan Lagorio. "Soros Sees No Bottom for World Financial 'Collapse.'" *Reuters*. February 21, 2009. http://www.reuters.com/article/businessNews/idUSTRE51K0A920090221.

Delaney, Arthur. "Al Franken: Foreclosure Paperwork Scandal Shows Need To Strengthen HAMP." *Huffington Post*. September 23, 2010. http://www.huffingtonpost.com/2010/09/23/bogus-affidavits-ingmac-_n_734742.html.

Delaney, Arthur. "Dems To Fannie Mae: Why Are You Feeding Foreclosure Mills?" *Huffington Post*. September 24, 2010. http://www.huffingtonpost.com/2010/09/24/house-democrats-to-fannie_n_738280.html.

Eckholm, Erik. "Prolonged Aid to Unemployed Is Running Out." *New York Times*. August 1, 2009. http://www.nytimes.com/2009/08/02/us/02unemploy.html.

Evans, Mark. "Is John Roth Home and Free?" *All About Nortel*. February 11, 2006. http://www.allaboutnortel.com/2006/02/11/is-john-roth-home-and-free/.

Farrell, Nick. "Indian Outsourcing Too Expensive." *Inquirer*. August 25, 2005. http://www.theinquirer.net/inquirer/news/1040943/indian-outsourcing-too-expensive.

Felberbaum, Michael. "Congressional Panel Examines Circuit City Bankruptcy." *Richmond Times-Dispatch*. March 11, 2009. http://www.timesdispatch.com/rtd/news/local/article/CIRCGAT11_20090311-163002/229000/.

Fletcher, Michael A. "Recovery's Missing Ingredient: New Jobs."

Washington Post. June 22, 2009. http://www.washingtonpost.com/wp-dyn/content/article/2009/06/21.

Fresco, Jacque. *Zeitgeist: Addendum.* Interview by Peter Joseph. (GMP, 2008) http://vimeo.com/13770061.

Froomkin, Dan. "A Convenient Truth: Gearing Up for Climate Change Could Supercharge the Job Market." *Huffington Post.* September 28, 2010. http://www.huffingtonpost.com/2010/09/28/a-convenient-truth-gearin_n_741430.html.

Froomkin, Dan. "'America Needs Jobs' Idea No. 1: A Payroll Tax Holiday." *Huffington Post.* September 21, 2010. http://www.huffingtonpost.com/2010/09/21/payroll-tax-holiday_n_732179.html.

Froomkin, Dan. "Job Creation Idea No. 8: Time for a New WPA." *Huffington Post.* October 8, 2010. http://www.huffingtonpost.com/2010/10/08/america-needs-jobs-time-f_n_754859.html.

Froomkin, Dan. "Job-Creation Idea No. 10: A Lower Dollar Would Level the Playing Field." *Huffington Post.* October 15, 2010. http://www.huffingtonpost.com/2010/10/15/jobcreation-idea-no-10-a-_n_763862.html.

Froomkin, Dan. "Job-Creation Idea No. 11: Buy American—If You Can." *Huffington Post.* October 25, 2010. http://www.huffingtonpost.com/2010/10/21/buy-american_n_771211.html.

Froomkin, Dan. "Job-Creation Idea No. 12: Let the Old Folks Retire Early and Make Way for Young Workers." *Huffington Post.* October 25, 2010. http://www.huffingtonpost.com/2010/10/25/jobcreation-idea-no-12-le_n_773391.html.

Froomkin, Dan. "Job-Creation Idea No. 13: No Better Time Than Now to Build The Future." *Huffington Post.* October 28, 2010. http://www.huffingtonpost.com/2010/10/28/jobcreation-idea-no-13-no_n_775265.html.

Froomkin, Dan. "Job-Creation Idea No. 2: Rescue the States." *Huffington Post.* September 22, 2010. http://www.huffingtonpost.com/2010/09/22/jobcreation-idea-no-2-res_n_734460.html.

Froomkin, Dan. "Job-Creation Idea No. 3: The Joys of Retrofitting."

Huffington Post. September 23, 2010. http://www.huffingtonpost. com/2010/09/23/jobcreation-idea-no-3-the_n_736271.html.

Froomkin, Dan. "Job-Creation Idea No. 7: Drawing a Line With China." *Huffington Post.* October 1, 2010. http://www.huffingtonpost. com/2010/10/01/drawing-a-line-with-china_n_746596.html.

Froomkin, Dan. "Job-Creation Idea No. 9: Encourage Banks to Lend—Or Else" *Huffington Post.* October 12, 2010. http:// www.huffingtonpost.com/2010/10/12/job-creation-idea-no-9-en_n_759329.html.

Froomkin, Dan. "Sharing the Pain of Layoffs Means Losing Fewer Jobs." *Huffington Post.* September 29, 2010. http://www.huffingtonpost. com/2010/09/29/work-sharing-layoffs_n_744302.html.

Garofalo, Pat. "SEC Chairman Christopher Cox Finally Realizes the Problem with Deregulation." *The Wonk Room* (blog). *Think Progress.* September 24, 2008. http://wonkroom.thinkprogress. org/2008/09/24/cox-deregulation/.

Goldberg, Steven T. "Robert Shiller Suggests a New Deal-Style Solution to Unemployment." *Kiplinger.* September 21, 2010. http://www. kiplinger.com/columns/value/archive/robert-shiller-suggests-a-new-deal-style-solution-unemployment.html.

Goslett, Miles. "I Just Can't Live with That Camera—It's Not Square … Inside the Bizarre World of £30bn Pyramid Schemester Bernie Madoff." *Mail Online.* January 3, 2009. http://www.dailymail. co.uk/femail/article-1104748/Inside-bizarre-world-30bn-pyramid-schemester-Bernie-Madoff.html.

Gross, Mathew. "The SEC Did Nothing on Madoff." *Deride and Conquer* (blog). December 20, 2008. http://mathewgross.com/2008/12/the-sec-did-nothing-on-madoff/.

Hamilton, Walter. "'Sorry' Is Not Enough, Madoff's Victims Say." *Los Angeles Times.* March 13, 2009. http://articles.latimes.com/2009/ mar/13/business/fi-madoff13.

Heller, Joseph. *Catch-22.* NewYork: Simon & Schuster, 1966.

Hilsenrath, Jon, Serena Ng, and Damian Paletta. "Worst Crisis Since '30s, with No End Yet in Sight." *Wall Street Journal.* September

18, 2008. http://online.wsj.com/article/SB122169431617549947.html.

Hiltzik, Michael. "How Could Savvy Investors Have Been Fooled by Madoff? Easy." *Los Angeles Times*. March 16, 2009. http://articles.latimes.com/2009/mar/16/business/fi-hiltzik16.

Ho, Chua Kong, and Bernard Lo. "U.S. Bailouts Add to Risk of Depression, Rogers Says (Update2)." *Bloomberg*. March 17, 2009. http://www.bloomberg.com/apps/news?pid=20601087&sid=a3kTp0KUJWWE&refer=worldwide.

Horowitz, Andrew. *The Daily Show*. Interview by Samantha Bee. Comedy Central. March 16, 2009.

Huffington, Arianna. "Larry Summers: Brilliant Mind, Toxic Ideas." *Huffington Post*. March 25, 2009. http://www.huffingtonpost.com/arianna-huffington/larry-summers-brilliant-m_b_178956.html.

"Insider Trading—What's the Problem?" CBC Online. December 21, 2005. http://www.cbc.ca/news/background/crime/insider_trading.html.

"IOSCO Technical Committee Members' Initiatives Relating To Restrictions on Short Sales." International Organization of Securities Commissions. October 2, 2008. http://www.iosco.org/news/pdf/IOSCONEWS129.pdf.

Jefferson, Thomas. *Memoirs, Correspondence, and Private Papers of Thomas Jefferson, vol. 4*. Randolph, ed., 1829, pp. 285-288.

Joseph, Peter. *Zeitgeist: Addendum*. http://vimeo.com/13770061. USA: GMP, 2008.

Katsnelson, Alla. "Research Loss in Pfizer-Wyeth Deal." *The Scientist*. October 16, 2009. http://www.the-scientist.com/blog/display/56063/.

Krazit, Tom. "Report: Apple Executives Faked Stock Option Documents." CNET News. December 27, 2006. http://news.cnet.com/2100-1014_3-6146011.html.

Krugman, Paul. "Rewarding Bad Actors." *New York Times*. August 2, 2009. http://www.nytimes.com/2009/08/03/opinion/03krugman.html.

Lamont, Owen A., and Jeremy C. Stein "Aggregate Short Interest and

Market Valuations." NBER Working Paper No. 10218. *National Bureau of Economic Research*. January 2004. Accessed November 1, 2010. http://www.nber.org/papers/w10218.

Lear, Norman. "Come, Shoot the Messengers!" *Huffington Post*. March 19, 2009. http://www.huffingtonpost.com/norman-lear/come-shoot-the-messengers_b_176692.html.

"Lou Dobbs Tonight—Exporting America." CNN. Accessed March 7, 2011. http://www.cnn.com/CNN/Programs/lou.dobbs.tonight/popups/exporting.america/content.html.

Loyd, Linda. "Pfizer Details Wyeth Deal." *Philly.com*. Accessed March 28, 2009. http://www.philly.com/philly/business/20090328_Pfizer_details_Wyeth_deal.html.

"The Madoff Files: Bernie's billions." *Independent*. January 29, 2009. http://www.independent.co.uk/news/business/analysis-and-features/the-madoff-files-bernies-billions-1518939.html.

Mazur, Robert. "Follow the Dirty Money." *New York Times*. September 13, 2010. http://www.nytimes.com/2010/09/13/opinion/13mazur.html.

McCullagh, Declan, Erik Lie, and Randall Heron. "FAQ: Behind the Stock Options Uproar." CNET News. July 26, 2006. http://news.cnet.com/FAQ-Behind-the-stock-options-uproar/2100-1014_3-6098457.html.

McIntyre, Douglas. "The Layoff Kings: The 25 Companies Responsible for 700,000 Lost Jobs." *DailyFinance*. August 18, 2010. http://www.dailyfinance.com/story/the-layoff-kings-the-25-companies-responsible-for-700-000-lost/19588515/.

McNish, Jacquie, Janet McFarland, and Paul Waldie. "Securities Watchdog Pursues Record Fine for RIM Execs." *Globe and Mail*. January 22, 2009. http://www.theglobeandmail.com/report-on-business/article967898.ece.

McPeak, Charles J. "Consider the Pros and Cons of Expensing Stock Options—Thinking Twice about FASB's Proposed Standard." *Graziado Business Review* Volume 5, Issue 4 (2002). Accessed November 10, 2010. http://gbr.pepperdine.edu/024/options.html.

Mitchell, Mark. "Manipulating Gold and Silver: A Criminal Naked

Short Position that Could Wreck the Economy." *Deep Capture*. April 2, 2010. http://www.deepcapture.com/manipulating-gold-and-silver-a-criminal-naked-short-position-that-could-wreck-the-economy/.

Montgomery, Lori. "Power of Stimulus Slow to Take Hold." *Washington Post*. July 8, 2009. http://www.washingtonpost.com/wp-dyn/content/article/2009/07/07.

Mostrous, Alexi. "More Families Are Becoming Homeless; Largest Increases in 2008 Came in Rural and Suburban Areas, Study Finds." *Washington Post*. July 12, 2009. http://www.washingtonpost.com/wp-dyn/content/article/2009/07/11.

Nasiripour, Shahien. "New Proof Wall Street Knew Its Mortgage Securities Were Subpar: Clayton Execs Testify." *Huffington Post*. September 25, 2010. http://www.huffingtonpost.com/2010/09/25/wall-street-subprime-crisis_n_739294.html.

Neumeister, Larry, and Tom Hays. "Madoff Sent to Jail as Furious Victims Applaud." *Huffington Post*. December 3, 2009. http://www.huffingtonpost.com/2009/03/12/madoff-arrives-in-court-f_n_174194.html.

Obama, Barak. "Building Something Better." *Washington Post*. July 12, 2009. http://www.washingtonpost.com/wp-dyn/content/article/2009/07/11/AR2009071100647.html.

Parker, Jennifer. "Krugman: U.S. Headed for 'Jobless' Recovery." ABC News. July 1, 2009. http://abcnews.go.com/ThisWeek/Politics/story?id=7966402&page=1.

"Peter Schiff on CNN World February 1st 2009." *CNN World*. February 1, 2009. http://www.youtube.com/watch?v=CXLgVJhVqPw.

Read, Madlen. "Stocks Rally on Good News for Banks, GM, Retailers." *Huffington Post*. March 12, 2009. http://www.huffingtonpost.com/2009/03/12/stocks-mixed-after-jobles_n_174242.html.

Robb, Greg. "Fed Crosses Rubicon and Sets Off Firestorm." *MarketWatch*. March 19, 2009. http://www.marketwatch.com/news/story/Fed-crosses-rubicon-setting-off/story.aspx?guid={CC678D54-22B8-4E39-8F0B-13A24308E7E8}.

Roberts, Dan. "Germans Are Not Posturing on Short-Selling: They're

Deadly Serious." *guardian.co.uk*. May 20, 2010. http://www.guardian.co.uk/business/dan-roberts-on-business-blog/2010/may/19/viewpoint-german-short-selling.

Satow, Julie. "Jim Cramer Shorting Stocks, Manipulating Markets, Saying the SEC Doesn't Understand." *Huffington Post*. March 11, 2009. http://www.huffingtonpost.com/2009/03/11/jim-cramer-shorting-stock_n_173824.html.

Schiff, Peter. "Credit Card Cancer." Euro Pacific Capital Inc. March 13, 2009. http://www.europac.net/externalframeset.asp?from=home&id=15698&type=schiff.

Schiff, Peter. Interviewed on Fox News. December 31, 2006. Accessed March 19, 2009.

Schiff, Peter. Interviewed on *Kudlow & Company*. CNBC. August 28, 2006. Accessed November 13, 2010.

Schiff, Peter. Interviewed on "More for Your Money." Fox News. Circa 2006. Accessed March 19, 2009.

Schiff, Peter. "Peter Schiff's Five Favorite Gold & Silver Mining Stocks." Euro Pacific Capital Inc. Last accessed November 27, 2010. http://www.europac.net/special_report/peter_schiffs_five_favorite_gold_silver_mining_stocks.

Schiff, Peter. "Precious Metals Investment Strategies." Euro Pacific Capital Inc. Last accessed November 27, 2010. http://www.europac.net/Precious_Metals_Investment_Strategies_1.

"A Science Odyssey: People and Discoveries." *PBS.org*. Accessed September 25, 2010. http://www.pbs.org/wgbh/aso/databank/entries/bhpavl.html.

Scott, Alec. "The $2-Billion Man." *Toronto Life*. Originally published April 2009. http://www.torontolife.com/features/2-billion-man/.

Sebert, Lagan. "Road to Ruin: Mortgage Fraud Scandal Brewing." *American News Project*. May 11, 2009. http://americannewsproject.com/videos/road-ruin-mortgage-fraud-scandal-brewing.

Sjuggerud, Dr. Steve. "Gold Stocks: 2 Ways to Size Up Investment Buys." *Investment U*. September 20, 2005. http://www.investmentu.com/IUEL/2005/20050920.html.

Springsteen, Bruce. *The Daily Show*. Interview by Jon Stewart. Comedy Central. March 19, 2009.

Stewart, Jon. *The Daily Show*. Comedy Central. March 16, 2009.

"Stock Dilution." *Trading Stocks Guide*. Accessed November 10, 2010. http://www.tradingstocksguide.com/investing-stocks/stock-dilution.php.

Summers, Lawrence H. "Testimony before the Senate Committee on Agriculture, Nutrition, and Forestry on the CFTC concept release—RR-2616." *US Department of the Treasury*. July 30, 1998. http://www.ustreas.gov/press/releases/rr2616.htm.

Taibbi, Matt. "The Big Takeover." *Rolling Stone*. Accessed March 19, 2009. http://www.rollingstone.com/politics/story/26793903/the_big_takeover/print.

Tapper, Jake. "Clinton: I Was Wrong to Listen to Wrong Advice Against Regulating Derivatives." *Political Punch* (blog). ABC News. April 17, 2010. http://blogs.abcnews.com/politicalpunch/2010/04/.

Tett, Gillian. "Insight: A Matter of Retribution." *Financial Times*. September 3, 2009. http://us.ft.com/ftgateway/superpage.ft?news_id=fto090320091244573891.

Tucker, Diane. "The Naked Untruth: Overstock.com CEO Patrick Byrne Hoodwinks DailyKos Diarist." *Huffington Post*. Accessed March 11, 2010. http://www.huffingtonpost.com/diane-tucker/the-naked-untruth-ceos-de_b_173754.html.

"US Rules on Abusive Short Selling." BBC News. July 27, 2009. http://news.bbc.co.uk/2/hi/business/8171667.stm.

"SEC Halts Short Selling of Financial Stocks to Protect Investors and Markets." US Securities and Exchange Commission. September 19, 2008. http://www.sec.gov/news/press/2008/2008-211.htm.

Vashistha, Atul. "Lou Dobbs Tonight—Exporting America." Interview by Lou Dobbs. *CNN*. July 27, 2009. http://www.youtube.com/watch?v=N1ohZET0qR8.

Vonnegut, Kurt. *Player Piano*. New York City: Charles Scribner's Sons, 1952.

Weidner, David. *The Daily Show*. Interview by Samantha Bee. Comedy Central. March 16, 2009.

www.ingramcontent.com/pod-product-compliance
Lightning Source LLC
Chambersburg PA
CBHW032019170526
45157CB00002B/762